Dumb Athlete

A MEMOIR

I0085246

Dumb Athlete

A MEMOIR

How My Biggest Fear
Became My Biggest Motivator

Chris Sain Jr.

CDS Publishing

Printed in the United States of America

3 2 1   4 5 6 7 8 9 10 11 12

www.chrissain.com

Special discounts on bulk quantities are available to public schools, charter schools, church youth groups, juvenile detention centers, correctional facilities, high school athletic departments, college athletic programs, professional sports organizations and other associations.

Unless otherwise indicated, Scripture quotations are taken from the *Holy Bible*, New International Version.

ISBN-13: 978-0-6159-8288-5

ISBN-10: 0-6159-8288-3

www.chrissain.com

Book Cover Photo by Britney Townsend

B. Townsend Photography

Cover Art by Charles Anderson

Chris Sain
#21 DB
Height: 5' 9" **Weight:** 176
Age: Young and Dumb
Born: 7/17/1983
College: All About Me Univ.
Class: Freshman
G.P.A. 1.89

dumb

[duhm] adjective, -er, -est, verb

adjective

1.

lacking intelligence or good judgment; stupid; dull-witted.

2.

lacking the power of speech (often offensive when applied to humans): a dumb animal.

3.

temporarily unable to speak: dumb with astonishment.

4.

refraining from any or much speech; silent.

5.

made, done, etc., without speech.

ath·lete

[ath-leet]

noun

A person trained or gifted in exercises or contests involving physical agility, stamina, or strength; a participant in a sport, exercise, or game requiring physical skill.

Viewpoints from current and former athletes about the *Dumb Athlete* Perception:

Carlton Brewster
College: Ferris State University
Professional: Green Bay Packers, Denver Broncos, New Orleans Saints, San Diego Chargers

"First of all, teachers always made examples out of us athletes. Because you are the talk of the school athletes stand out, but as soon as you make a mistake teachers will put you on blast in front of everyone. Being an athlete, when you win, you get the glory, but when you lose you will hear about it. It's a love lost situation. But everyone can't be an athlete. It's a blessing to be an athlete. Dumb athlete is a stereotype. Ivy League schools have the best academics in the country, and athletes are at those schools. Athletes are in high class power, you have some who own businesses, have political power, and are professors. Athletes are the talk of the town."

Thomas Kelly aka T.K.
College: Michigan State University
Professional: Basketball – Hungary –Soproni

"Perception! People perceive athletes to be a certain type of person! The sport is what we do, not who we are as individuals! Especially the STAR athlete! You get labeled a lot of the time! People watch what they do and if you fail, it is talked about. I don't think people understand the hard work and discipline we had to put in to be good at our craft. The long hours of practice and the extra work on your own time to be good at it! On top of that, being a good student! Like I tell kids all the time, academics and sports goes hand in hand. You can't have one without the other especially if you are trying to go far in sports. It's an honor and privilege to be put there performing!"

Terna Nande
College: Miami of Ohio
Professional: Tennessee Titans, San Diego Chargers, Indianapolis Colts, BC Lions

"The stereotype of athletes being called "dumb jocks" has become the norm in today's society for multiple reasons. The first reason is often equated to athlete's low academic performances in the classroom. I believe that athletes are not the only ones to blame for this issue. Many times athletes do get special privileges because they are talented in a sport but generally most people don't hold them accountable for getting a proper education. Athletes are exploited and only praised when they are able to entertain crowds. Everyone is a part of this growing epidemic because when it all boils down to what we as people value the most education isn't at the top of the list. Last time I checked, hundreds and thousands of people weren't packing a stadium to see a math or science competition. I was taught the value of education at a very young age. That education is the one thing no one can ever take away from you and the more you know the more powerful you become. I wanted that power and to achieve greatness on and off the field."

"The second reason I believe athletes get bad reputations are because everything that most athlete do gets magnified hundred times more than average person. Media outlets have created this monster, therefore giving the perception that most athletes don't make good decisions. It's a double standard society has enforced on athletes. No one can understand the pressure placed on athlete's day in and day out unless they are athletes.

"The term "dumb Jock" is not a state of mind for most athletes but a mind state of oblivious average people that will never know what it takes to be an athlete." - T. Nande

Corey Gonzalez
College: Saginaw Valley State University
Professional: Saginaw Sting

"Well from the start of my playing career starting at little league my dad and other coaches installed in us at a young age that education is first and sports second. So that stuck with me for my whole entire playing career. That motivated me to become a great player on and off the field where I'm not perceived as the dumb athlete but the student first athlete who got a degree from a four year university."

Eze Ejelonu
College: Michigan State University
Professional: Saginaw Sting

"Before beginning my football career in the 11th

grade, I was guilty of labeling the stereotype of athletes being dumb. I failed to realize that athletes endure and overcome more challenges on and off of the playing field/court then other students that are not athletes. Outside of personal challenges, athletes are given a role to play that ultimately affects the lives of coaches and their careers. Therefore the pressure is high. It was not until I became an athlete myself and learned how to balance my responsibilities as a man and student that I finally understood the life of those athletes who refuse to settle and make something of themselves by rising above all challenges and most importantly being able to give more than what is minimally required academically. People fear what they don't know and would rather read the cover of a book rather than its pages.

Mark Miller

College: Saginaw Valley State University
Professional: Saginaw Sting

"Although I was always a great athlete since the age of 8 my mother always said that school came first. When I was a freshman in college my uncle who was a college basketball player told me "Don't leave the university until I get my degree. Throughout my whole college career I remembered those words. I came from a family of scholars so a high school diploma wasn't good enough."

Serenity Prayer

God, grant me the serenity to accept the things I cannot change;

Courage to change the things I can;

and Wisdom to know the difference.

<u>Dedication</u>

To all those who made a decision to be more than what society expected and predicted…

I also dedicate this book to anyone who has been labeled, anyone in bondage to the limitations placed on you by others.

To rise above the expectations of evil, your environment, the world and to live *in* purpose, not *on* purpose is the greatest achievement of them all.

Contents

PREFACE

The Day It All Changed

Sometimes we lose our way. That is exactly what happened to me. After surviving a poverty stricken environment, violence and death, I was supposed to write a book to tell the world about it. Instead, I graduated with my Master's Degree and lost sight of the vision and eventually lost control of the wheel. I wrote this book at seventeen (17) to tell about how I made it to eighteen (18) in an environment where very few reach that age alive. It took a life changing event, a freak accident, to serve as a reminder of what I was expected to do. My journey almost turned out to be The Greatest Story Never Told.

February 20th, 2011 – The day it all changed

Sunday, @ 8:37 a.m.

James 4:14 best describes my near tragic experience. "Life is but a vapor," which is a paraphrase of James 4:14. It was a gloomy morning. I was off to somewhat of a late start given the amount of travel time needed to arrive at work on time. No time for breakfast, I hopped in the car and begin to roll. Listening to T.I's No Mercy album I was determined to make it to work on time despite the elements I was faced with. Rain, hail and snow covered the pavement. My daily commute was an hour to and from work. I traveled the 80 / 90 Toll Road. I often found refuge in my car. My car served as a place for me to decompress and reflect. I worked primarily with adjudicated youth. Many came from low-income families and very poor communities. Daily I listen to heart wrenching stories from adolescent youth. February 20th I was running a little late. I prided myself on being punctual, reliable and dependable. I was going faster than normal on Interstate 80 /90 knowing that it took me about a solid hour to make it to work. I often talk to myself when I am alone. Positive self-talk and affirmations helps me mentally prepare for things to come in the workplace. This day was no different. Alone in my car, I remember saying to my "Man, these roads are a little slick and it's windy out. I must avoid all slow cars and semi-trucks in order to make it on time." When I first merged on to the toll road I felt a strong wind against my car. I paid it no mind. I believed at the time that my hands were not firmly placed on the steering wheel.

As I headed down the toll road trying my best to make it to work on time, it continued to rain. The weather was a mess that day. There was a mix of rain, hail, sleet, light snow, black ice and strong winds. It was the perfect combination for what took place that morning. I drove a 2003 SAAB 9.3 Linear. The car was both sporty and sophisticated. I thought it represented who I thought I was at the time. That particular make and model is nice but very small. The SAAB was no match for the strong winds present on that morning. Riding mainly in the right lane, I wanted to get a feel for the highway and the severity of the winds. I am a defensive driver so I often allow enough space between my vehicle and others on the road as well, as I look ahead for potholes, police, deer's and black ice. Pressed for time, I thought I had the road which I travel daily figured out. I had been making this commute for over two years. I successfully made it through a tough Indiana winter in 2010. I thought I had it figured out. I began to increase my speed. I could not afford to be late. We just implemented a new attendance policy at my job and I was already off to a bad start.

Looking back, I remember this day as if it was yesterday. In need of a quick maneuver around a semi-truck that was driving very slow as well as kicking up lots of rain onto my windshield I made my move. The roads were not the best and overall conditions were poor but I looked in my rearview and over my shoulder and my path was clear. I accelerated enough to generate speed to transition over to the fast lane also known as the left lane. As I put my blinker on and began to cross over I remember a strong wind grabbing ahold of my car causing it to go in a direction I did not intend for it to go. I quickly turned the steering wheel very rapidly toward the right hand lane. The wind would gain more strength, slick roads and black ice did not help. The strong winds took my SAAB from the right lane to the left lane, off the highway and into a ditch. My car flipped over as it headed for the ditch. I was now upside down in the middle of a ditch. Thank God for my seatbelt but it had entrapped me. I was unable to release myself. My windshield was shattered. My car was upside down. After gathering myself and calming down I was finally able to free myself from the seat belt. Once released, I fell onto the windshield causing it to shatter a bit more. Everything inside of my car was now dispersed on various parts of the roof which was the floor now that my car was upside down.

I was stuck! For nearly ten minutes which at the time seemed like a lifetime, I was stuck! My door would not open. My car was still on. I began to think about the many movies I saw where vehicles catch on fire. I thought my car was going to catch on fire. I was stuck and unable to free myself. My window would not raise-down and down in the ditch it prevented my doors from opening. I was stuck! For a brief moment I thought about my legacy and what it would be in the event my car burst into flames and I was unable to escape. That thought lasted only a brief moment. The fact that I was not already dead gave me enough hope and it let me know that the Lord's covering was over my life. The rain and light snow continued to fall. It was a messy day. Still stuck upside down I heard voices. Three separate individuals pulled over to pull me out. They asked was I alright and contacted the ambulance. Rainy, muddy and cold they tried prying my door open. They were unsuccessful. I began to think "You mean to tell me that three decent size men are unable to pry this door open?" They continued to pull and use their strength until they were able to jar the door open. The rain continued to pour. The passenger side window went down a little but not enough for me to climb out. It was up to the three individuals to get the door open. The rain made the grass in the ditch soft and muddy. The door began to slide open. It was now open far enough for me to climb out. I was free! I was free!

Unscathed I looked around as the rain drops fell on to my face. I thanked the three gentlemen who came to my rescue. Without their help, I'm not sure if I would have been able to get out. Each individual ask if I was okay. I assured each of them that I was okay. One had already contacted the Emergency Medical Services (EMS). They arrived within two minutes of me being free from the car. The three gentlemen, whose name I never got, returned to their vehicles and drove away. EMS had arrived. While they were making their way over to me, I called my job to inform them what had happened. Trying to avoid being late, I was not going to make it in at all. EMS began asking me a set of standard questions: "Are you okay? Do you need medical attention? Anyone else with you says the officer? Any sign of a headache?" I answered No to all his questions. He later expressed relief that I was alive and unharmed. He saw how bad my car looked sitting upside down in the ditch. He told me that I was the sixth car that morning that held fell off the road and into a ditch. He said I was lucky. I said I was blessed. He informed me that I may begin to experience some aches and pains later and that because of my adrenalin, I was probably masking any serious injuries at the time. A police officer arrived and he also asked me a series of medical questions. His questions were similar to the EMS worker. The officer had paperwork for me to complete as I sat in his is car trying to gather myself. I was wet and cold. My mind was all over the place. Inside my car I carried many important papers. My car was my mobile office. I had many important documents that were not retrievable and being destroyed by the rain. The papers the officer had me fill out were consent that I was denying medical treatment. My signature suggested I was declining medical attention.

Without transportation, the officer drove me to the nearest exit and took me to a local gas station. The nearest exit was exit 77 South Bend / Notre Dame. While driving, he told me about the other sixth vehicles that had slipped off the road and into a ditch. Some were not as fortunate as I was. While driving I looked out the window and sure enough I saw four of the six vehicles including an Uhaul that had slipped into the ditch. The officer graciously drove away. Now, inside the gas station I asked the cashier for a phone book. I needed to call a tow truck to retrieve my car but more importantly I needed to retrieve the classified information and paperwork inside my car. My car also serves as my mobile office for my non-profit organization. Everything is done online and in the car. After securing a tow service company, I called my auto insurance company. At the time I thought "Thank God for auto insurance." They took care of everything from there. I called my Fiancé. She didn't answer so I sent her a text. My text read "My car flipped over, I'm at the gas station. Come and get me." She thought I was joking around and shortly after she called. Once I answered and she could tell I was not joking, she became frantic. "Where are you? Are you okay? I'm on my way." She was at work at the time. Her job was across town so I knew it would take at least 20 minutes for her to arrive. While waiting for her, I called my mom. I sent Carlton, my best friend a text and both my brother's. I took a picture of my car while at the scene. I sent it to their phones. My boys always think I'm joking so the picture was proof that I was not joking

A natural worrier, my mom did what any mom would during that moment. After I told her what happened she asked her series of questions. She said; "What happened? Are you okay? Did you call your job and tell them what happened? Do you need to go to the hospital?" I knew when I called my mom she would have a grocery list of questions. I answered each of her questions calmly and respectfully. I think she could sense I was upset about the entire accident by the tone of my voice. Those that know me well know that I am very tidy and organized. For the most part I try my best to avoid setbacks and things of this nature. I planned on going to work. I had plans for the weekend. My money was already accounted for and I knew what I wanted to do with my money. My nice, neat life was being interrupted and it was a major inconvenience. I was also a Grand Rapids Public School Board Candidate at the time and had several appearances to make and doors to knock on. I was now without a vehicle and my peace and serenity was being interrupted. My mom said you sound upset are you okay? I said yeah, I feel okay. I'm not injured or anything. She said well you sound upset. I thought about what she said for a short moment and replied "I am upset. I'm mad this happened. I'm hot. All of my important papers were all over the car and the rain was destroying all of my documents plus my car is probably totaled." My mom said "Lil Chris, none of that matter's. Those things don't matter. The fact you are alive is all that matters. We can get another car or C.D's and papers and other things you are complaining about but we can't get you back. Those other things can be replaced, you can't." Moms' was right. It was during that moment that I realized what she was saying was the truth and all that really mattered in that moment. I could replace my car and most of the items that were lost or destroyed in the accident. If I had lost my life during that moment, there would have been no way to get my life back. Mom was right. The picture of my car flipped over in the ditch made its way to Facebook. Sometimes you don't know the impact you have on others or how much you mean to others until something tragic happens. The Facebook comments and post really said a lot to me. I was touched by the response and all the heartfelt messages from my Facebook Family. Mom was right, I couldn't say it enough but she was. Her comments made all the sense in the world.

My fiancé at the time had finally arrived. Her only concern was me and my health. She did not once ask about the car. Mom was right. My life is all that mattered to my loved ones. No one was concerned about the SAAB. No one cared about all of my C.D.'s or so-called important papers. I sat in the passenger seat quietly and reflected. I had questions. I was still confused about all that had happened. Everything happens for a reason but why God? I was searching for a reason. I wanted answers. We made it home safely. Everything felt surreal. I went to the bathroom and looked in the mirror just to make sure I wasn't dreaming. I had no aches. I had no pains. If I had a vehicle, I believe I could have actually gone to work. But I stayed home. My Fiancé had to return to work. I sat in my computer chair reflecting. I kept asking why. I kept looking for reasons why the Lord allowed this to happen. I was thankful he spared my life. Although I was not injured, I took a couple of days off from work. I very rarely take days off from work, so the time to myself was nice. Most of the days while at home, I sat around and thought about why. I started throwing different things around in my head. I replayed previous days, weeks and months. I looked for every clue possible. Did I do wrong by someone? Was I disrespectful toward someone? Questions continued to enter in and out of my head. Finally God spoke to me. I soft voice whispered "I needed you to slow down, re-evaluate why you are doing the things you are doing."

At the time of the accident, I was working at the Berrien County Juvenile Center located in Berrien Center, Michigan. I was working at the University of Notre Dame which is conveniently located in South Bend, Indiana. I was also commuting back and forth to my hometown of Grand Rapids, Michigan where I conducted business for my own nonprofit organization called Grand C.I.T.Y. Sports, Inc. while running for the Grand Rapids Public School Board. Last but not least, I was engaged. My commute to and from work was approximately 54 minutes daily. It's safe to round that off to the nearest whole number. I was very active in my home town although I did not physically live there. I lived approximately 80 miles or the equivalent of a hour and a half away, give or take the flow of traffic. Once I stopped or should I say, once the Lord stopped me, I was able to look at how I was spreading myself thin by trying to be all things to all people as well as do too much. The message was clear. God simply wanted me to be still. Settle down, reprioritize and allow him to order my steps. Instead, I was out trying to win *"man of the year"* and lost focus of my purpose. God has a way of getting your attention. On February 20th, 2011 he placed my car in a ditch, totaled and un-repairable, ruined all of what I considered important just so I would have to sit and be still. The Lord had no intentions of harming me. That is why I came out that horrific accident unscathed. He just wanted to get my attention. Jesus wanted me to allow him to lead the way. Without the accident, who knows if I would have ever stopped and sat down to actually type the chapters to my story? I'm not sure I would have.

INTRODUCTION

"An individual has not started living until he can rise above the narrow confines of his individualistic concerns to the broader concerns of all humanity."
~ Martin Luther King, Jr.

Not all legend is about victory. Sometimes it is about the struggle. Dumb Athlete is a story about the first twenty-four years of my life. Many days I wondered if I'd live to see eighteen! Life in the inner-city is unpredictable and growing up in the inner-city there are no guarantees. I believe that everyone has a story. I knew at the age of seventeen that I wanted to one day share my story, but I waited, hoping I would make it to eighteen before deciding I actually would. See, many predicted that by eighteen but, for certain by twenty-five those of us who grew up in the inner-city would be dead or in jail. My friend, who lived two or three houses down from me was shot and killed at the neighborhood corner store when I was thirteen, so at times, living to see eighteen didn't feel realistic. The cycle of poverty is real. There are people in the *Land of the Free* that are uneducated, on welfare, homeless, on drugs, see no future, believe they are meant to be imprisoned, view violence as the only resort to solving problems and afraid to be anything. Once I survived those extreme conditions and outlived those predictions, I began to write. Writing was actually easy because in my head I had already visualized the entire book. I've always enjoyed writing. For me writing was a coping mechanism. Although I am reluctant at times to share my life, my story is intended to inspire and inject hope into people, young and old, from all walks of life on things I did to defy social norms and worldly expectations. So when people ask why I chose to write a book to share my story, I simply respond; "WHY NOT?"

"You haven't lived enough to write a book, let alone a memoir. What experiences have you had?"

"You are too young to write a book."

"Who do you think you are? You are not famous, who do you think will read, let alone buy your book?"

"It's not like you are a celebrity or anything. You don't even have a platform."

"What are you writing a book for? Your generation doesn't read."

To those who speak and feel this way, I say; "WHY NOT? You have a story to tell as well. You should think about sharing it."

For as many people who pose as haters and naysayers, there are just as many that ask;

"Chris? How did you turnout okay when many of your friends fell off?"

"Can you speak to the students in my classroom? They need to see someone who looks like them that made it."

"You have grown up to be a good example and such a wonderful young man. How did you come out different?"

"I didn't have much hope for your generation, but something about you was always different."

Before we begin, I want to make sure we understand the point of this book. This book is not about sports or football. Sport's is great. Football in particular is great. It is the ultimate team game and it teaches many life lessons. Football gave me hope, it gave me a dream. It gave me something to shoot for and served as my ticket out of my neighborhood by putting me on the fast-track to success. It was the only thing that got me excited and allowed me to come out of my shell. I am naturally quiet. Many that know me can attest that outside of football, I might not speak ten words the entire day, but while playing ball, I noticed I was a different person, more outgoing, loose, and alive.

There is more to life than football…but not much. Football is just a game. It is not more important than my relationship with God or my family. It does not add value to my life although it has taught me many things about life. For over 18 years football defined who I was. When my dreams of playing professional football fell through, it forced me to find out who I truly was, who God intended for me to be. I realized during my darkest hour that football is what I do, not who I am. I realized that I was blessed with far more gifts than just playing ball. It is important to understand it is the journey that matters.

With sports, football in particular, runs parallel with life. It teaches you how to win and lose. It helps build character through adversity and challenges faced. It is a brotherhood that teaches you about togetherness, community and selflessness. In sports, you have to persevere and be resilient just as you do in life. It teaches discipline as well as sportsmanship, which are skills also needed to be successful in life. So again, it is not about sports or football. It is about the journey and how the lessons learned inspired me to touch lives, be an advocate for change and an inspiration to a generation that lacks inspiration, leadership and hope.

Today "there are over 400,000 college athletes and almost all of them will turn "Pro" in something other than sports." Today there are also over 1.6 million people in prison in the United States. Growing up in the inner-city of Grand Rapids, Michigan South East side it was often said that I would be dead or in jail by twenty-five. I attended Grand Rapids Public Schools and graduated from Ottawa Hill's High School in 2001. My senior year I thought to myself, I'm not dead or in jail but at the time I graduated from high school over 1.9 million people were in prison. Determined to prove the media and other naysayers wrong, I went to college. If nothing else, I thought college would provide me an escape from the drug infested streets surrounding my neighborhood.

As a first generation college enrollee, I was taking my public school education to an institution of higher learning, a four year university. Without question I experienced my share of ups and downs. Grand Rapids Public Schools best effort could not have made me college-ready. My teachers were great, well most of them but too many external factors played a critical role in the learning and development of urban youth. I was not college material. In college, just to get by, just to keep up, I relied heavily on tutors, office hours, peer study groups and good looks to charm my professors, at least the female professors. With male instructors, I relied on prayer. I was naturally articulate and well versed. I think those attributes helped as well. College football and men's basketball players are dramatically less likely than other students to obtain a degree. By 2008 I was able to do the unthinkable. I accomplish something that very few African Americans have. At the time, I was twenty-four. On the other side of my story was the stark reality. A reality that is more consistent with African American males today. Like many I grew up with, I was supposed to be dead or in jail by twenty-five remember! As of June 30, 2008, over 2.3 million inmates, or one in every 131 U.S. residents, were held in custody in state or federal prisons or in local jails according to the Department of Justice. I guess for some adults and media outlets, their predictions were right about many, especially African American males. They just weren't right about me! Many in my community said I wouldn't amount to anything, many believed I would be dead or in jail, not just me but my peers as well. The media and local news portrayed African Americans as criminals. We are often associated with negativity, the negative things that happened in the community, the violence.

Maybe I was naïve, but I never paid attention to any of what was being said about me or things I should not or could not do. Although I read the newspaper, watched the local news and heard what people said about me and my generation, I always assumed they couldn't possibly be referring to me. Growing up, I was not afraid of becoming one of the young-black-males headed to prison. That was not my fear. Unknown to many, I knew what prison was all about. I spent over half of my life visiting Michigan State Prisons also known as Correctional Facilities. I had an older brother who at the time was serving twenty-five (25)-to-Life before his sentence was later reduced to eighteen (eighteen (18) to twenty-five (25) years in prison. It is never easy for any family when you have a loved one incarcerated but I was not afraid of repeating my brothers' mistakes or falling victim to the drugs, gangs or crime in my neighborhood. A silent code of respect had been established in my neighborhood and throughout the urban communities. I was not sure when and how it was established, but it was. I guess it is safe to say what's understood does not have to be said. I was an athlete! I was not trying to be nor was I interested in being a street guy or dope dealer. It is said that, real-recognizes-real. I believe the statement to be true. Although the inner-city is unpredictable and random acts of violence can visit anyone, I never a day in my life worried about personal attacks or gang violence approaching me. Many of the guys that comprised of the neighborhood gangs also known as sets or cliques were at a point and time, childhood friends, acquaintances, classmates or little league teammates. Guys knew me. They knew what I was about.

Not to be confused for what today's society and urban culture calls lame or square, guys in the street knew what time it was. Many of the individuals who identified as *"street"* or *"thug"* or *"hard"* approached me with a great deal of respect and admiration. Others who were not as familiar kept their distance opting to mean mug and stare in hopes of a cowardly reaction or a show of weakness. With the uncertainty of inner-city life and unpredictable behavior of lost boys armed with guns and poison (drugs) I was aware that there still was some risk just merely living-in and around drugs and crime. But yet, I was still not afraid. Faced with overwhelming odds and social determinants that continued to suppress our low income impoverished community, I was more afraid of being called dumb, a dumb athlete. My fear of that two letter word nearly blinded me to all that was wrong with the world, my city, my neighborhood, my school system and the African American community.

The journey should be the focus as you read along *Dumb Athlete*, not football or making it out of the inner-city alive. If it were all about making it out of my neighborhood or the cycle of poverty, I would have stopped the minute I determined I had arrived. This book is not about me. It is about the choices and decisions, the mindset and approaches that led to experiencing truc success. It is about "us" you and me together, overcoming and knocking down barriers. It is about using your story for his Glory, turning your mess into a message and turning your pain into Praise. It is to help others to stop looking for handouts and approval from others and begin to strive for greatness and excellence. I hope that when you finish with this piece of literature you understand it was never about me and every bit about the Lord's Grace and Mercy.

Childhood

I remember when I fell in love with football. I was seven (7).

I remember my favorite team then was the Bengals because of their tiger striped helmets. Tigers are my favorite animal. I remember visiting my oldest brother in prison.

I remember my mom and dad arguing every holiday.

I remember walking to Mini-Miti but known as Miti-Mini after school.

I remember hearing my mom and dad arguing before church on Sundays.

I remember in elementary school looking forward to going to Ottawa Hills High School Varsity Basketball games with my mom.

I remember playing with my wrestling men and using them to form a football team.

I remember lying in bed and hearing my mom and dad arguing.

I remember hearing the ambulance and fire truck sirens every night. I remember hearing my neighbor across the street from my house fighting in the street with his girlfriend. I remember my mom coming to tuck me in at night and I would pretend I was sleep.

I remember going to church on Sundays. We would stop by the gas station and buy peppermints.

I   Chapter 1

__Dumb Athlete__

Biggest Fear and Motivator: An Athlete Perspective

The Lord doesn't see things the way you see them.
People judge by outward appearance, but the Lord
looks at the heart.
I Samuel 16:7

"Be Good at everything but, be Great at
something." ~ My Dad

Everything in the universe begins with and revolves around and is given life & energy by two things: Thoughts and Words. Thoughts and Words are the two things that drive the substance and existence of all things therefore I must guard what I say and I must guard what I speak because what I say and what I speak and what I think is what I become. Thoughts and Words form the creative substance that fills molds and shapes your destiny. I now wear the Helmet of Salvation to protect my mind from negative thoughts because it is negative thoughts that would derail God's plans and purpose for me.

Sport's is often the primary way a kid from the inner-city expresses himself. When a kid from the inner-city is asked "what do you want to be when you grow up?" often the answer is a Basketball or Football Player. Sport's becomes our escape. For some of us, it becomes our way out of the inner-city. We focus so intensely on being the best, we forget to live. Education then becomes secondary. Athletes resent studying and doing homework because it is thought that one could use that time to shoot 100 extra jump shots or get a lift in. The title Student-Athlete is often a misrepresentation. It misrepresents how the athlete actually views himself. Use football and basketball for instance. Athletes identify themselves as a football or basketball player, while many fail to realize football and basketball is what you do, not who you are.

Martin Luther King Park is where I honed my skills. Football and Basketball was my life. As a kid I never traveled out of state. I barely traveled outside the city limits of Grand Rapids, Michigan. The only place I had ever been was Muskegon, Michigan. Most of my family on both my parents side lived there. Lucky me! I wondered what other places were like but after a while it no longer mattered. I went to King Park. That was my get-a-way. *King* was my sanctuary. It was also 2 minutes away from my house. As I walked up the street toward the park, with either a football or basketball in my hand, I would say to myself "*I will be better than my competition.*" Self-talk began early for me. I made myself believe that while other kids my age were out on summer vacation and spring break they were only having fun, while I remained home, continuing to push myself and improve my skills. Other inner-city kids were around. Their families did not have the means to travel or take vacations either. That reason alone is why I worked even harder. Most neighborhood kids carried the same chip on their shoulder, but those who believed ball was our way out worked harder than others. When football and basketball season would come around I would play with a chip on my shoulder. It bothered me that as a family we never traveled or went on vacation the way my white classmates did. I took my frustration out on my opponents. I made myself believe that going places such as trips and vacations really didn't matter. I would tell myself that those other players, especially white kids, didn't put in the work I did all summer, they were most likely traveling, or at Cedar Point and Disney World. I used actual games to show them how much better I was. I wanted my play to reflect the work I put in during the summer months. I felt twice as good as my peers on the court and on the field, mentally and physically. One reason I felt this way is because King Park attracted a tougher more aggressive crowd. Street guys, neighborhood kids and gang members would hang out and play ball there. According to the streets, *"choir boys"* had no presence at King Park. After playing against them, and eventually dominating them, school kids became less of a challenge. The mentality was different at school, than at the park. At school, sports were organized. You had coaches and referees. At the park, it was about surviving, earning respect and competing. There was no coach around to play favorites and fouls did not exist.

In 1997, I entered Ottawa Hills High School. It was clear that when it came to sports, I was a natural. In my first high school football game, I scored four (4) touchdowns. I played running back, cornerback, punt return and kick return. We played East Grand Rapids (EGR). East witnessed me score three (3) rushing touchdowns and one (1) Kickoff return. East at the time represented a school that had players with parents who had the means to take regular vacations. I scored at least three (3) touchdowns every time we played them up through my sophomore year. Junior year, I had a breakout year at corner. I had 11 tackles, two (2) for losses against a tough EGR team. By the time I was a senior, they knew what I was capable of. East would not kick the ball off to me on kickoffs and they loaded box on defense. With that type of early success, it was now just as important for me to perform well in the classroom. That East game got everyone's attention. I knew they were watching! I would go on to score at least three (3) touchdowns in the next two games as well. I accumulated season ending numbers by week four of the season. I took pride in being as good on the field, as I was off of it. I continued to push myself. The attention was nice but I also knew how important it was to lead by example. My coaches would say "Chris, you are one of those kids we (coaches) don't have to worry about. You are a coach's dream." Nice gesture, but I don't know about being a coach's dream, but I did know they never had to worry about whether I had the grades to play. More importantly, I didn't have to worry about if I had the grades to play. I completed homework and school assignments. For me, it was a way to at least know I would be able to perform on Friday nights. Our breakfast luncheons recognized top performing students. I never wanted to be left out of breakfast luncheons held for students with good grades. That was my biggest fear. Not being in attendance would have revealed my biggest secret. In high school, I created a façade, one of great confidence, and overall I was, but I feared being called a "dumb athlete" which in turn, motivated me to go the extra mile to achieve academic excellence in the classroom. During middle school, that was not the case.

I attended Iroquois Middle School. I was ruled academically ineligible to play basketball my 8th grade year due to poor grades. Skipping class and trying to impress my peers who were doing the same caused me to get off track. 7th and 8th grade was around the time that smoking weed and having sex was the popular thing to do among my peers. Peer pressure and the temptations of my environment were powerful. I earned a 1.8 Grade Point Average (G.P.A.). I let a lot of people down, including myself. Being ineligible was embarrassing. I was starting to make a name for myself as a basketball player at the time. I was afraid I was also making another name for myself as well. It was a feeling that I never wanted to feel again. It was difficult facing my peers each day. It was more difficult facing the girls and trying to explain to them why I'm not playing this year. I did not attend any games that year. I couldn't. I was hurt and the pain I felt would not let me go toward the gym. I did however show up to class every day. I completed extra assignments and dedicated myself to my studies. I wanted to at least enter high school on a positive note. I vowed to never be ruled academically ineligible ever again. I feared being recognized only for my athletic ability and being perceived or called a "dumb athlete."

Deep down inside I felt inadequate when people, particularly teachers would ask "what do you want to be when you grow up?" I would always respond, "Go to the NFL or NBA." That was the easiest response to give. That response allowed teachers to move on to the next student which got me out of the hot seat. Honestly, I did not have any real life examples to model my life after. My dad worked and eventually started his own business but I was too young to really truly understand the business he was building. No one I knew was a doctor or lawyer, and in the inner city we had very little contact with those types of individuals. Professional Football or Basketball Player was the safest answer. It was the only thing familiar to me. As I got older, I strived to find a better answer for teachers when asked about my future. I struggled. Playing ball had really become my passion, not to mention I was really good. My coaches say I was a "natural." Deep down inside I felt like adults, especially teachers came to expect that answer from African American boys. I felt they asked the question hoping to hear something different but expecting to hear Football or Basketball Player.

Although sports has been part of my life since I was eight years old, I've always viewed it as a means to do something more. I believed making it professionally would give me the means to encourage and uplift others. It would give me the platform and notoriety needed to make a difference. I struggled to convey this message to my teachers and other adults who would ask. I felt I was putting myself in a box every time I said something about playing ball. I was mad at society and my environment for not exposing me to more. Drug dealers and gang members never intrigued me, yet they had the most representation in my neighborhood. I was always told that opposites attract. Never quite understood why as a kid, but found it to be true. See, most dealers and gang members liked my style. Many would choose a different path in life, maybe one similar to the path I appeared to be on but selling drugs often provided the only income for themselves and their families. I think they understood I was not easily influenced, nor was I impressed with that lifestyle. My desire to live Christ-like drove me toward righteousness although I was a Carnal Christian at the time, plus, my father was also present in my life and in the community. I'm sure that had something to do with it as well. I know it did. Overall, respect was mutual. Til' this day, I stay away from politics due to the majority of my friends having felonies. Politics is a dirty game. My friendships are far more important to me than being a politician. Politics scold you for knowing or befriending someone with a criminal history. I also have no political aspirations. I write all of my friends and from time to time, send money to the ones doing time in prison. Many convicts no longer have a name and are more commonly known by their number, the prison ID number each inmate is issued. I happen to know a side of some of them the penal system will never know, and for that reason I remain loyal.

Being a natural athlete came with its share of downfalls. One downfall was that coaches did not have to spend as much time with me. I assume it was because they did not need to. But, what most of my coaches beginning with Rocket League and throughout high school failed to realize is that, the lack of attention in some ways hindered my overall growth and social skills as an athlete and a person. The same thing can be said for my school teachers. In the classroom I was quiet. I was not a disruptive kid. Teachers often dedicated most of their attention to the other students, students that were disruptive or had behavioral problems. Sitting quietly in class, I was irritated. I started to feel the downside of being a natural athlete and a good student. For me, it was not worth it. The two biggest influences in my life at the time outside of my parents were constantly focusing their time on others. On some levels I felt neglected. I felt inadequate and now I began to feel incomplete.

My mother and father made up for how I felt. They always encouraged me to do my best. They were always there for me. They attended conferences and other school functions but more importantly to me, they never missed a game. From Rocket League Football throughout my High School Sports career, they were there. My mom and dad made up for what I missed from my teachers and coaches. I was blessed to have both parents in the home as a kid. Being quiet and behaving myself made it easy for my parents to get me the best of everything. I wished we would have done more as a family, but the latest shoes and video games made up for it all. Ironic I thought. How could the same behaviors have different results? I know my teachers and coaches were helping others but growing up, I felt overlooked. The more touchdowns and baskets I made the less attention I got from my coaches. I remember saying to myself "this is backwards." I felt the lack of attention from coaches and teachers led me closer to achieving the "dumb athlete" status. I felt shallow. I felt the relationships that should be most meaningful were becoming meaningless. I guess that's the price you pay for being a good athlete and a good student. It just felt backwards to me.

During high school I tried to put forth the same amount of effort in the classroom as I did on the field. It was about balance. As a kid, I remember going to high school basketball games and wondering why certain players on the team were in "street clothes." I remember watching College Football on Saturday mornings and listening to analyst talk about players that would not "dress" due to academic ineligibility. For some reason, out of all things discussed by sports analyst, points about not dressing or will-not-travel always stood out. For me, I understood how demanding sports could be as well as the sacrifices made when trying to be great, so when I heard players, good players, were ruled academically ineligible, I thought to myself "that could be me" and in the 8th grade it was.

It takes a special, dedicated and focused individual to perform at a high level on the field and in the classroom. When sport's is your passion as well as your ticket out of your current environment, education takes a back seat. Once the 2.0 GPA is obtained, not much effort is put into becoming an advanced learner and doing what it takes to be a scholar-athlete. As an athlete, my focus was often on getting my family out of the hood, buying my mom a car and a big house. When you get home from school and you are faced with gangs, drugs, domestic violence, drive-by shootings, and the sound of ambulance sirens constantly throughout the night, survival becomes your number one priority, while education, studying and reading becomes that much more difficult.

Many teachers have no clue what a student's home life is like. Many teachers today do not live in the school district in which they work which is a huge problem, especially in our Public Schools. Teachers, not all, but some are out of touch. When a student shows up to class, it is often assumed that we are or should be ready to work. In reality, we are hungry and looking forward to 8 hours of sleep. The things faced in the home, then at the bus stop, and in the school hallways has most students' minds far from learning. Even two parent households had its share of problems.

There is a huge misconception about kids growing up in a two parent household. Family discord and dysfunctional marriages has a way of affecting a child that often gets overlooked in school if the child is not displaying behavioral problems or acting out. In the public eye my parents looked like the model couple. I remember seeing how people in the community reacted to my parents when they saw them out in public or at a game. They had no clue of the problems my mom and dad faced in their marriage. The ability to present as a unified front out in public helped them keep the façade going. "Chris, we love your mom and dad, they are such a beautiful couple." That is what my peers and other adults said to me on a regular basis. I use to respond with a simple, "Yes they are." Deep down inside I realized how deeply fooled they had everyone. I turned the other cheek. At least I was fortunate enough to have both parents was my thinking. My closest friends did not have a clue. I guess you can say my mom and dad was good at making things look okay. Living in the home, I knew differently. I've seen and heard a lot.

When I was in school, the Zero Tolerance policy was introduced which was followed by the No Child Left Behind Act. Both policies showed me how out of touch government officials were in relation to urban schools and urban communities. I remember sitting in class and watching my friends get in trouble. Some were kicked out of school while others received an in-school detention. As I watched my peers be removed from class, I also knew what some of their home environments were like and the challenges they faced before even stepping foot into the school. Teachers and School Officials had no clue what they were doing. To suspend and send a kid back home to an abusive environment or one that lacked food and water was the last thing students wanted. The majority of kids that grow up in the inner-city are resilient. We endure things that most adults, especially teachers would not believe before 7:00a.m. Just getting to school was a blessing.

My situation was not the best but it was not nearly as bad as others. Playing ball was my escape. Playing ball was the way I coped with society and an environment that was filled with negativity. I wished I could have provided teachers a better or even more educated response when they asked me what I wanted to be when I grew up, but the truth of the matter is, football and basketball kept me alive. As an urban youth, survival is option number one, two and three. This is why sports meant so much. Football and basketball kept me away from drugs, gangs and out of harm's way. My dream of playing professionally was my motivation and it gave me something to shoot for. College became part of my reality because it was my path to the pros. As a kid, Florida State University (FSU) and the University of

Michigan (U of M) were my schools of choice. I woke up every Saturday morning to watch "College Game Day." As a kid from Michigan, to play ball at Michigan was the goal. Having that goal early on in life gave me hope. It let me know something more and something better was out there for me.

Some kids did not have a vision. The inner-city is designed to kill your vision. In the inner-city, many kids parents are in and out of prison, some never get out, so it was easy to understand why. Some kids did not see a way out. Prison was the path most family members took, so for some, prison was at least in the plans. Some kids would tell teachers they hoped to play professional football or basketball when they grew up but some knew that was not a reality. That's the difference. For me, it was a realistic goal that I believed was attainable. Things I did outside of school, on my own time made it a reality for me. I made sacrifices along the way and I expected those sacrifices to payoff down the road. I completed high school. I stayed away from trouble. I graduated near the top of the class. I excelled in football and basketball. To my surprise, my senior year, my classmates voted me "Most Handsome" and "Most Athletic." I looked back and thought about all the teachers who asked me what I wanted to be. I told them all I wanted to play football or basketball when I grew up. The difference between my peers with the same goal was that, I was willing to do whatever it took to be great. I made sacrifices and dedicated myself to being great.

Just me and my little brother

Born 16 months apart was my little brother, my better half. His name was Preston. Today we call him G.C. short for Gold Child. That name actually fit him perfect. That name represented exactly what he was. His life experiences were similar to mine. Everything I saw, he saw. Everything I experienced, he experienced. As kids we were all we had. When friends were not around, or over to the house, it was just me and him!

Many thought we were twins. I tell him all the time there is no way we are twins, he has always been far better looking. More photogenic, talented, smart and gifted in multiple areas, G.C. always did his own thing. As my little brother, part of my responsibility was to look after him, make him tough. My dad would not have it any other way. He sat me down at an early age and instructed me on what my role was as the oldest.

G.C. was naturally tough however; he had to work a little harder to reach his potential as an athlete. Although we are 16 months apart, I was two grade levels ahead of him. Since a kid G.C. grew up around older guys including me and my friends. Well versed in the streets, he also became a great athlete. One of the best in his class, he played Varsity Football as a sophomore. Always around better athletes growing, by the time he hit high school, he was better than half of the players on Varsity. As my little brother, I wouldn't have it any other way. I was driving when G.C. arrived to high school so; his high school experience was a lot different than others. He rode to school every day with me. I was already a household name in the school so in turn, everyone knew him as well. He was also popular apart from me, so being in the spotlight came easy for him. In addition to sports, G.C. was an exceptional student, especially throughout the years. Although he appeared to lose focus down the stretch during his senior year, he graduated on time before eventually transitioning to a music artist. As kids we spent all of our days together and to this day, we talk almost every day.

Thank God for 'Madden'

It might sound crazy to some, but I thank a video game for playing a part in saving my life. Between 'Madden' and NBA Live on PlayStation kept me and some of my closest friends out of harm's way and on the right track. My best friend Carlton Brewster (C.B.) and I would wake up every Saturday morning and the phone conversation went like this: C.B. at 8:00 a.m. - "What up? You trying to see me in that Madden?" or "You want that rematch?" From that moment on, that's what we did. Between 8:30 a.m. until 10:30 p.m. We would play Madden. Then, when basketball season came around, we switched to NBA Live. Between both games, we had some intense battles. Some battles even got heated. We were so competitive controllers were thrown, buttons were broken followed by screams of "They cheating" or "He can't do that in real life." G.C.

and C.B had their share of battles as well. Eric Malloy, my other best friend witnessed every game. He didn't play much but would get a kick out of watching the arguments each game generated. Everybody hated losing. A.J., Darryl Folden and Sergio Pinto, three of my other good friends were also gamers and brought their competitiveness over to the house. The rivalries in both games gave us something to look forward to.

II   Chapter 2

P.O.M.E.

Product of My Expectations

Never let the conditions of your environment or your past, dictate your future

For I know the plans I have for you, declares the Lord, plans to prosper you and not to harm you, plans to give you hope and a future.
Jeremiah 29:11

On the road less traveled you very rarely see people like yourself

One day I overheard individuals talking and what appeared to be a group discussion among educated professionals the statement was made that;

"Many African Americans (Males) who are overcome by drugs, street gangs and lack of education are products of their environment."

I've always believed I was a product of my expectations. Not sure where the belief came from, but I have always expected to be great. Born and raised in Grand Rapids, Michigan, I honed my athletic skills at Martin Luther King Park and received my education through Grand Rapids Public Schools; the same Grand Rapids Public Schools that many believe are failing today's youth.

It is my belief that 90% of failures come from people who have a habit of making excuses. When speaking throughout the Midwest, the one thing I share with all youth is to go after what you want in life. You control your own Destiny and the journey alone is your success story. Everything comes down to Choices & Decisions. Your Decisions determine your destiny.

For as long as I can remember, every one of my accomplishments started with a decision to try. I often say, to do *good*, you actually have to do something. One cannot be afraid to fly. A person has to be willing to take risk or at least calculated risks. My dad, when I was a boy, always told me to set goals for myself and write them down. He said to always make sure they were visible so that I could see where I was going. Finally, the last thing he would say was, make sure your goals are realistic and attainable.

This made me aware of the fact that it did not take sight to reach the top, it took vision. Because of goal setting, my life is simplified. I have set priorities for myself. I did not always know where I was headed, but I was certain of where I wanted to be. I learned and began to realize that the most valuable commodity in the world was information and in order to get to where I planned to be, I had to make informed decisions, I had to be knowledgeable. The Bible says *"our people are destroyed from lack of knowledge."* - Hosea 4:6

I believe you get out of life, what you expect out of life. Never let your past, dictate your future and never use the conditions within your environment as an excuse. We are all products of our expectations, so expect to be great and expect to be the best. Expect to graduate from high school and expect to go to college. Remember to set the bar high because society has already set the bar low. By the 3rd grade a determination has already been made about kids' futures. Researchers say failing schools are pipelines to prison. One could conclude that maladaptive 3rd graders are expected to end up in prison. I believe that through mentoring, pro-social peers, adults and activities as well as increasing protective factors, improving housing conditions, that same 3rd grader could be our next Doctor, Lawyer or President.

"By twenty-five you will be dead or in jail…if that" was the mantra when I was growing up and it is what many say about today's youth. To some degree, I actually believed that statement when I was growing up. I remember when my sixteenth birthday arrived, I was relieved. One of my best friends was shot and

killed when I was thirteen. That was 1997. James 4:14 says "Life is but a vapor." The New International Version reads; *"Why, you do not even know what will happen tomorrow. What is your life? You are a midst that appears for a little while and then vanishes."* His name was Derrick. He lived a couple houses down from me. When he was shot and killed, and because his house was literally a couple houses down from me, his death hit so close to home, I thought death was around the corner for me as well. Death felt like it was two doors down.

Derrick was my neighbor. Derrick was my friend. We walked to school together. We played ball together. We slap boxed together. We played video games together and did all the things kids who grow up too fast do. He was my friend and he was no longer here. The dead or in jail mantra felt as real as it had ever during that time. In August of 2000, I lost another close friend. His name was Eddie Vander. He was in Atlanta for the summer and died in a car crash. We grew up together, played ball together and chased girls together. He was sixteen at the time of his death. Making it to my eighteenth birthday was feeling more and more unrealistic. My senior year would not be the same without Eddie. Unfortunately, this was just two of many more deaths I would endure during my teenage years and young adult life. *"Do not let your hearts be troubled. Trust in God; trust also in me."* – John 14:1. Putting my trust in the Lord is exactly what I did for a short time.

I graduated from Ottawa Hills High School in 2001. I was seventeen. Our Freshman Class came into High School full of hope and somewhere along the way our paths began to define it-self. I lost many friends along the way. Some of us grew apart. Some were locked up. Others died. Part of me felt like I outlived expectations, I was not dead or in jail, yet at-least, and, I was enrolled in college. I set new expectations for myself, now that God's grace had spared my life. It was time to live, besides, it was said that I'd be dead by now. Everything I sat out to do did not happen as planned but at least I was alive. I played Division I College Football. I worked toward a Bachelor's Degree and was racing against time to do it all before I was twenty-five. As a first generation college student, if I earned my degree, I'd be the first to do so in my family.

I now had new expectations. In my mind, I've already won, at least for the time being. I was supposed to go to jail or dropout of school or have six or seven kids by four or five different baby mommas. Society said I would not make it out alive. My environment presented obstacles that I was not supposed to overcome. The devil continued to set traps. I defied those odds. I've already won. I now expect to be the best at whatever it is I choose to pursue. I expect to one day be a good husband and a loving caring father to my first child. But regardless of what happens, I've already won. I expect to complete my dissertation. I expect to challenge men who have taken the day off to be present. Since I am still alive, why not be the change I expect to see? I was young. I was cocky. I was eighteen. Who doesn't know it all at eighteen? But, I was still within the window for the naysayers to be proven right. Making it to twenty-five was the goal. Have you figured out, making the right choices isn't always easy, but it's always necessary? I had seven years to go.

Part of me felt I could not lose. I felt I had already won. I am a product of my expectations not my environment. Resilient and perseverance; two words that describes me best. I opted for the right thing instead of what was popular. Doing the right thing is not easy. It never has been easy to do right when faced with the temptations of society. To do wrong is a lot easier. Many choose the easy way out. It is easy to smoke when everyone around you smokes. It is easy to take or steal from others when you don't want to work for it. It is a lot harder to work to earn what you want. Many choose *Easy Street*. Easy street is often a one way street that comes to a dead end eventually. Pushing the bag, commonly known as selling weed, does not offer a retirement plan. It does however ensure you a spot in one of the newly built federal prisons or county jails. Taking calculated risks can sometimes lead to setbacks or a total loss. But at least the opportunity to bounce back is present. Taking penitentiary chances is a risk that has a much more severe consequence.

We are trained by each other to not achieve. Our environment predicts that at best, we will sell drugs and be violent toward each other for a living. Our environment, the inner-city, is not conducive to learning and prefers we act outta control. The less education we have in our environment the less we are likely to succeed. The liquor stores on our corners are meant for you to drink your life away. The dope fiends and crack heads in our neighborhoods are there to show you what you will be in five years. The easy access to firearms and ammunition are meant for you to kill your neighbor and then kill yourself. Abusing drugs causes you to be dependent and mediocre; it gives you an excuse not to be more. Learn to avoid the traps that are in the environment. Be better than what your environment predicts you will be. Refuse to be a product of your environment and choose to be a product of your expectations. I'm from the hood. I come from the same environment exploited on the nightly news every day and night. The difference, I expected to make it out and be something more. I've often said, I'm far from hood, but I understand the streets. I understand that the streets can hold you back if you let it, so, break free from bondage and be more.

Who am I?

What is your purpose? What do you believe your purpose on this earth is? Why do you do what you do?

I think it is important to ask yourself those questions. I think ones answer to those questions is even more important. People who live life with a purpose tend to live a much more productive life. The quality of life is enhanced because their life's work is dedicated to their purpose. But be careful. Don't confuse your desires, for the purpose God has for you. Many of us pursue things that we were not led to by God. Be sure to let God lead the way. Allow Him to order your steps and trust that he will see you through. Your purpose should supplement your relationship with God.

Purpose produces wellness, sustainability and growth. When we feel good spiritually, we feel good naturally. Your purpose is designed for you to be fruitful. Be on your guard. Do not allow someone to talk you into your purpose. Remember, God has to do the advancing.

As a kid growing up, I was not sure where I was headed. All I knew was that I wanted to play football. I had no plan-b or nothing else to fall back on if football did not work out. Although I had no direction or neither a sense of what I was or who I was, I did know that I aspired to be somebody. And because I knew early on that I wanted to be somebody I became very intentional about the type of person I wanted to be. Fortunately, I had my father in my life and he helped model certain things that helped point me in the right direction. But I still did not know what I was or who I was or wanted to be. Many of you are chasing a look of success, status and money. I too am guilty of this. I chased a look of success, but really did not know what success was really all about. I chased status but again, I did not know what status was about. I chased money and only knew of one legit way to obtain it.

The way we were portrayed on television led me to believe that success meant being on T.V. Men on T.V. tend to be upholding an image, a *look* of success. Now that I am much wiser, I now see that most of those men who are before us on the T.V. screen are really miserable. They spend all day reinventing them-selves, hoping to appeal to the world. Status, to me meant having the most girls. Having the most girls gave me status. I referred to myself as a *Playa* or *Player*. People thought I was "the man" coming up. I remember guys as early as Elementary and during Junior High and High School being envious of how I attracted the girls. People, my classmates, coaches, school officials and even men in my neighborhood associated me with having all the "pretty girls." Now that I am much wiser, I was nothing more than a womanizer. Because I was young, dumb and foolish, I thought I was actually doing something. I was chasing status in the form in which I saw it displayed in my environment. Money - Outside of my parents giving me money, the only way that I believed I would acquire money was through playing football. I did not believe in working a traditional job. I looked right past living examples of men and women working hard. My own parents were examples of hard workers, yet my ear accepted more of what I heard from the streets to be true. My environment said 9 to 5's don't pay enough. A traditional J.O.B meant *just over broke*. Some call us the microwave generation. We want instant gratification. Many are unwilling to work for what they want and go through life with a sense of entitlement. We lack patience and want it all right now. I was no different. I knew professional football players made millions. I thought I would make millions. Making millions would allow me to help out my family. I had a brother in prison who I wanted to be able to provide for once he returned home. I had the sweetest mom in the world and I wanted to buy her the house of her dreams and allow her to leave her job. I was looking for a get-rich-quick scheme and for me that was football. That was the NFL. I did not value work. The Good Book says; *"We can make our plans, but the Lord determines our steps."* – Proverbs 16:9

How did my outlook on work get so distorted? My mom and dad worked. My dad had his own business and was a successful entrepreneur. They were both hard workers and provided for me and my brothers. God intended for man to work. *"The LORD God took the man and put him in the Garden of Eden to* work *and take care of it"* - Genesis 2:15. How did my perception of work become so distorted? Work is what God intended for man to do. In Thessalonians 3:10 the Bible says *"If a man will not work, he shall not eat."* Big Momma put it plainly. *"If a man don't work, a man don't eat."*

Growing up my purpose was predicated on things I was exposed to. My purpose was not clearly defined. It lacked substance and a clear direction. I was a *Purpose-*

Resister. As men, we often delay our increase. *Purpose Resister's* are those who are delaying their increase because the earthly cost is too high. Growing up, I was more concerned with being too much like the world. How did I become like the world? I searched for answers but often came up with very little to justify my actions. 1Timothy 6:10 – *"For the love of money is a root of all kinds of evil. Some people, eager for money, have wandered from the faith and pierced themselves with many griefs."* It hit me. I had wandered from the faith and the proper steps to obtaining prosperity. I was chasing a look of success, status and money but unwilling to submit myself and discipline myself. I was calling my own shots and creating my own way instead of allowing God to order my steps and lead the way.

I was fighting two battles. My first battle was with society and my second battle was with myself. I was eager to prove society wrong. I was not going to end up dead or in jail by twenty-five. My life had a purpose, although I really did not know what it actually was. I refused to be another statistic. I refused to let their predictions about inner-city African American youth hold true. We are not products of our environment. My life had a purpose. It was up to me to figure it out. My second battle was an internal one. Trying to figure out how to make it out and be able to provide for my family, buy my mom a home and live the good life was the bulk of my second battle. My internal battle came to an end one day and it was after this passage sunk into my spirit; *"Trust in the Lord with all your heart and lean not on your own understanding"* – Proverbs 3:5.

Everything happens for a reason. Sometimes it is hard to figure out why certain things happen. It is even more difficult trying to figure out why bad things happen to good people. Some things I may never figure out. Some things are not meant for me to figure out. See, the natural mind is logical. God is not logical. Man cannot figure him out. *"And we know that in all things God works for the good of those who love him, who have been called according to his purpose"*- Romans 8:28. I was brought up in the church. I am thankful for being brought up in church although as a kid I did not understand what was being said or the intent of the message. I was too young to digest the teachings of the bible and trying too hard to be like the world. I'm currently in recovery. I'm in recovery of me. A Believer and being a Man of God has nothing to do with church membership. I am a Man of God. *What is a Man of God?* A Man of God is a Man of Purpose and a Man of Integrity. *What makes you a Man of God?* The answer is simple. Faith makes you a Man of God.

Perception does not always equal Reality

God has a plan for your life. It's true. It is important to make sure your plan, aligns with what God has planned for you. One must have vision. Remember, it doesn't take sight to reach the top, it takes vision. Vision helps outline where you want to go and who you want to be. It is a long-term view of your-self that concentrates primarily on the future.

Some will say one's perception equals one's reality. Although their perception equals their reality, it does not equal the truth. It is up to you to define your truth. A few words of advice to help break the cycle of hopelessness and poverty in urban communities as it relates to perception;

> Portray yourself the way you want to be perceived. Remember, hater's won't give you the benefit of the doubt. If you are a young person looking for work or currently have a job, it is important to dress for the job you want, not the job you have.

> You don't have to accept the world that was given to you. You can envision a better world for yourself.

> When you help others expect nothing in return. The Bible says "Each one must do just as he has purposed in his heart, not grudgingly or under compulsion, for God loves a cheerful giver." Your reward will come from God! Stop giving others reason to believe you are selfish and selfless. Deuteronomy 16:17 "Every man shall give as he is able, according to the blessing of the LORD your God which He has given you."

Going through something? Use your story for his Glory. Turn your Test into a Testimony. Turn your Mess into a Message. Finally, Turn your Pain into Praise.

You can't let other people tell you who you are. You have to decide that for yourself. So again, ask your-self, who am I?

Many of you are chasing a look of success, status and money. But ask yourself, how does that truly benefit you? How does that add value to your life? You must have long term goals to keep you from being frustrated by short term failures. I have failed at many things in my life. I failed and made excuses for why I failed. I remember trying to blame others for why things did not work out in my favor. I remember being concerned about what others had and what they were doing. I am now certain that being controlled by the opinions of others is a guaranteed way to miss what God's purpose is for your life.

Where we come from, Satan (the adversary) looks like he is on your side. We live fast and die young. That's the way we live and that's the way we view life. The adversary will open doors and even move things out the way for you. It will look like you are successful. Remember, perception equals reality but it does not mean their reality is the truth. The adversary will take you to the top, only to push you off.

We have all made mistakes and did things we are not proud of. Romans 3:23 - *for all have sinned and fall short of the glory of God,* but it is important to understand that our shortcoming do not define who we are. How you bounce back is far more important than how you fell off. Never let yourself be defined by your mishaps. True character is shown by your ability to go through something, not around it, standing tall and holding your head high. Who cares what you did in the past or what someone said about you? "You can't let praise or criticisms get to you. It's a weakness to get caught up in either one." That's what the great John Wooden said.

You can't be out here livin like you are scared to fail when you are already losing. Know whether you are chasing a dream or a fantasy. One is connected to purpose and the other to pleasure! Many have small minded and lopsided pursuits. Ask the next person you see how much money he needs to be satisfied with life and I'm sure you will hear something about a million bucks. Many want to be a millionaire but don't have a $100 in your bank account; therefore your perception does not equal one's reality.

During instances where perception actually equals reality, how about we thank God we don't look like what we've been through. Things that happen in life are not always because of Sin. In life, you will go through "Trials & Tribulations." *Young people are prone to foolishness & fads; the cure comes through tough-*

minded discipline. -Proverbs 22:15

My final few points regarding perception vs. reality are;

1. Stop ignoring your gift...your gift may just bring you before great men.

2. Don't brag about yourself — let others praise you. -Proverbs 27:2 / Let someone else praise you, not your own mouth--a stranger, not your own lips.

3. All the ways of a man are pure in his own
    eyes, But the Lord weighs the spirit. – Proverbs 16:2

4. You can't wait for people to get on board with YOUR vision!!!

5. Success is not a destination but a series of wise decisions along the pathway to discovering the best of the greatness in you.

When you get right with God, God's favor begins to look real good on you. Everybody wants to be around you. So, it's important to stay grounded. When you are right with God, the perception that others have won't matter because your gifts will describe you. "People will know the tree by the fruit that it bears", therefore they will know who you are and what you are about by what you do with your life.

III   Chapter 3

Michigan Department of Corrections
(MDOC)

My Second Home

> *You are not a number. You are a person.*
> ~ Chris Sain Jr.

"Imagine going through 19 calendars, 19 Birthdays and 19 Holidays in a 6 by 8"

Jay, my oldest brother had numerous run-ins with the law before finally being sentenced to 25 to life. His sentence was later reduced and he spent the next nineteen years of his life in prison. Although I was not physically inside the prison walls I felt like I did the whole nineteen with him. I wrote and visited him constantly. Throughout the nineteen years he bounced around various prisons in the state of Michigan. I became all too familiar with Jackson, Ionia, Bellamy Creek and Muskegon Correctional Facilities. Visiting my brother became a normal function of my daily life.

While most of my peers in college went home for the weekend or while they took a much needed road trip, I would travel to one of many state prisons to visit my brother. In high school it was the same thing. Middle school was no different. When I was in elementary school, it hurt to leave the visit. I was too young to understand why he would never leave with the family. Visits came with its set of rules. The rules insisted that family sit on a specific side and no hugging or he cannot get up to get food, only guest and family can move around or get food. I looked forward to the picture guy coming out. The picture guy was always another inmate and most of them took pride in their job as a photographer.

I remember being stripped searched and going through the metal detectors. I would always forget to put my belongings in the lockers located in the waiting area. Most guards were hyper-vigilant, they were always on edge. I hated taking my socks off. They checked everything. It felt like I had to nearly strip butt naked to have a visit. The experience was humiliating but I got use to it. It became part of the process. It was what had to be done in order to visit my brother.

Growing up it was hard at times not having my big brother around. His presence was missed. His absence created a wedge in the family. During holidays we would visit distant relatives and not having him around for those irreplaceable moments took away from the actual experience. Most of my peers, teachers and coaches never knew I had an older brother. These same individuals definitely did not know he was in prison.

You have a collect call: *15 minute conversations*

*"This is a call from the Michigan Department of Corrections. You have a collect call from"…*Jay.

For nineteen years I fielded calls from my brother. *"You have 1 minute remaining."* I thought to myself, where did the 15 minutes go? Since I was around eight years old, Jay was in and out of jail. As a habitual offender and a criminal rap sheet as long as Rodeo Drive, he was destined for prison. I missed not having him around. I missed him not being there. When I was young, he would call the house. He would ask, what's up? What ya'll doing? When I answered, I would give him a full rundown of what everybody in the house was doing. - "Bro? Momma gone. I think she took back some clothes to get enough money to go to Bingo. Preston chill'n. He upstair's playing the video game. Pops is gone too. He's been gone all day. He'll be back soon though." Jay would call and always check to see how everyone was doing. He would also ask about our Rocket League Games. I had to ball because I had to be able to say what my stats were and be confident that he would be impressed. The difficult thing was he was never there to actually see me play growing up. I think as a kid, I learned a lot having a sibling in prison. I realized that I cared for him just as much as I did those who I had access to every day.

Caller I.D. was just hitting the scenes. While away from home, I gained added comfort knowing that the caller id would give the family a good indication when Jay called. The caller id specify that an "unavailable" called was missed. 9 times out of 10 "unavailable calls meant that Jay had call. My little brother and I would hang around the house and kept a close eye on the phone when we missed his call. I remember actually being on the phone talking to my girl or various friends of mine when a call would come through. Once I saw "unavailable" I quickly clicked over. Sometimes it was bill collectors but often times it was Jay. The automated operator would say its speech and I remember leaving plenty people on the other line without clicking back over. His calls meant a lot to me. They were very important. I did not want to risk the chance of our call being disconnected by trying to click over. "This is a call from the Michigan Department of Corrections. You have a collect call from…"

Middle School and High School was much of the same. However, I realized that as I got older I began to live a little. My life was evolving. My anticipation of the calls was neutralized. I was often away from home. I was at practice, or I was trying to get-up with my girlfriend. I use to write letters consistently. I use to send pictures. I noticed a huge decrease on my part. See, nineteen years is a lot of years. That's many calendars. I was living. I was coming into my own. We would still talk. We would engage in very meaning conversations. My brother was a thought provoking individual. He spoke about everything with great substance. Jay was far from shallow. I was growing up.

I was popular and the type of kid that others wanted to be around and associate with. My friends took a lot of time away from what was most important. Family problems were also starting to emerge. My mom and dad often argued and had difficulty getting along. As a kid, I was happy they spent so much time away from home and away from each other. My mom escape was Bingo. My dad chose to bog himself down with work. There was peace in the home when they were not present. When they would return home you immediately felt the tension. The tension between my parents was so intense I stayed in position to be able to react in case something jumped off. It was hard to juggle all that was going on and still be the support Jay needed.

I remember my mom answering his calls and how she tiptoed around family discord. Jay's father was named Clyde. We had different fathers. My mom believed that if she told Jay that she and my dad were not on good terms, he would somehow be upset, and ultimately do something to my dad. Her intent was good, but long term she may have caused more agony. My mom also believed that by keeping family dysfunction away from Jay would allow him to avoid confrontation in the joint. Again, my mom intent was good. She always meant well. The actual result of how things played out is a different story. Although my mom strategically and secretly kept family problems away from Jay, I often felt her tone gave it away. She successfully kept things away from him for most of his

19 year sentence but I believe my brother made a conscious effort to not entertain the thought or inquire deeper. Many weekends were dedicated to traveling to the various prisons around the state of Michigan. After visits, we would all struggle with the reality of Jay not leaving with us. We would take pictures and hug as tight as we could. His letters and phone calls were all we really had to look forward to. The one thing about the visit is that, it reiterated how important the phone calls meant. For guys in prison, it seemed that the little things mattered so much more. It became ever so apparent when communicating with my brother. A letter, a picture or a conversation was enough to get him through the years.

For me, the most difficult thing for me as a kid was to follow my mom instruction. She truly meant well, but she would instruct Preston and I not to tell him what was going on at home. I thought to myself, why wouldn't she want him to know? I believe Jay, even from a prison cell could have offered the family the type of insight that would reduce our dysfunction. But see, that's the level we talked on. I knew he could help the situation. My mom felt otherwise and thought it was best we present as a unified front to assure him that things were ok. She felt being in prison was stressful enough. She did not want him worrying about us because if he did, he would find himself in more trouble inside the prison. Lucky for me, my brother never asked about family. He would mainly ask about me and how I was doing or how football or basketball was going.

With only 15 minutes to talk, my replies would take up the most of the time. Before I knew it, the operator would chime in to say "You have 1 minute remaining." When Jay would call, I would be so happy to talk that I honestly didn't think twice about our family problems. I was more interested in his day. Prison stories are often very interesting. Some are even funny. A lot of today's pop culture lingo originated in Prison. Even if I just listened on the phone for 15 minutes, I was sure to hear the new slang or a creative use of everyday words. I really enjoyed the stories about the arguments. Jay would re-enact disputes between individual's playing cards, basketball or on the yard. He would tell the story so vividly that it made me feel I was there. I laughed and laughed. It was comforting to know that guys were finding ways to survive. My brother helped me see that although they would not see the light for quite some time, they still had hope. He helped me see that even inmates knew how to laugh and make the best of their situation. Not all stories were sweet. He shared altercations, stabbings and other violent acts committed. Movies and T.V. shows has truly misled the masses.

Everything I did, I tried to capture for my brother. I now knew how important the little things were. In high school, I sent newspaper articles, homecoming pictures, swirl pictures and letters. It gave us a baseline for our next 15 minute conversation. I use to anticipate his call anxious to see had he received the items I sent. I could not wait to hear his response. His perspective meant a lot. I would be upset when football and basketball articles misspelled my name or used the wrong picture. I would often refrain from sending flaw material. I would have to speak to my successes or accomplishments when he called. 15 minutes were all we had. 15 minutes consisted of life happenings. Sometimes those 15 minutes were the most meaningful minutes of my day.

Now in college, the 15 minute conversations became more important. I was now away from home and so was my brother. College and prison was the distinct difference. I could sense my family keeping things away from me when I would call home. Every time I would call home and ask how things were going, my mom or dad, depending on which one answered would say "Everything is going good." I thought to myself, now wait a minute. I lived at home for seventeen years of my life. Never has everything been all good. I knew all too well my family and their ability to cover things up or make things sound better than what they truly were. I was away at college and though Michigan State was only 45 minutes away from home, I often felt I was thousands of miles away. Playing ball and living the life, Jay calls had added value when I was in school. See, I started playing ball at eight years old. By nine I was a star. I was a star for the next 10 years, none of which he physically witnessed. For the first time I was facing my own adversity. Football was not going the best, my athletic career was bleak.

Dumb Athlete

Practice ended and as most of my teammates headed over to training table. For me, things were much different. I hurried over to my dorm room, unlocked the door and headed toward my phone. I had no caller id, but the blinking red light indicated that I had a message. I would check my messages with anticipation of one of the calls being from the Michigan Department of Corrections. I would listen to the message all the way through to hear the exact time of the call. I would then look over at my alarm clock to see how long ago the call was. I would often forgo meals to ensure that I didn't miss his next phone call. Those 15 minutes were too important. I would hit up members of the Circle to grab me something to eat from the café, but I refused to leave my dorm.

No one at State knew me the way my brother did. When things were not going well, outside of my closest friends, Jay was the only person I felt comfortable talking to. It was obvious that Jay was intrigued by the college experience. During our conversations, he would ask about my classes, the class size, difficulty of assignments and the girls. See, football barely came up. His concern was with everything that wasn't football. We talked until the operator said "You have 1 minute remaining." Jay would hang up and call right back. It was almost like, we only had each other. I was gone and he was gone. College and prison was the only difference. Jay was academically astute and very scholarly. I would share with him class expectations, demands and requirements. I would read the class syllabus to him and ask for his viewpoint. I would even ask him for topic ideas and what to write about. Our 15 minute conversation became filled with substance. We did not waste a lot of time on irrelevant things. I remember one call in particular; Jay called and talked about sending me a piece of his writing. He was curious to see how his writing would measure up at an institution of higher learning. Jay reads a lot. He is very knowledgeable about many things including real estate, social injustice, religion and politics. Jay also writes a lot. The letters also known as "kites" that we exchanged are considered small scale writings. Grammar and sentence structure was his biggest concern. Based off of letters he sent me, I knew his writings would earn him high marks at any college. So for me, it was nothing. I told him to go for it. I encouraged him to send me some literature and that I would give it to one of my professors for review. He later sent me his essay. I check my mail days later and his writing had arrived. I read it first. I felt I needed to read it to first determine if it was worthy of me passing off to my professor. Once I began to read his writing, I became more and more engaged. He didn't just send a piece of fluff. This piece of work was thought provoking. Honestly, it was better than anything I had written during my time at MSU. I decided that I wanted my professor to take a look at my brothers writing. Much like Jay, I too became anxious to see what kind of feedback his writing would receive. Our 15 minute conversations proved that we were blessings to each other. We fed off each other's energy, ideas and vision. We developed closeness and we vicariously lived through one another.

Prison traps your body, not your mind

For many urban families, we know all too well about loved ones falling victim to the system, the penal system. Many of us have a loved one in prison or some sort of confinement and aside from the visits, are subjected to 15 minute collect calls. Despite the entrapment, the mind remains free. It's important to understand that prison only traps your body, not your mind. Think about others before us such as Gandhi, Nelson Mandela or Malcolm X. Nelson Mandela was sentenced to life in prison. He spent twenty-seven years in prison. Once released from prison, he became President of South Africa. Malcolm X was sentenced to ten years in prison. After seven years he was released. He fought for Human Rights. Malcolm X believed we could never get civil rights in America until our human rights were first restored. Malcolm X felt we'd never be recognized as citizens in America until we were first recognized as humans. He viewed racism as the cancer that is responsible for destroying America. Both Malcolm X and Nelson Mandela, once freed from prison, went on to accomplish great things but while entrapped, there mind continued working. Nelson and Malcolm are good examples of men of great integrity who persevered in their purpose. They strategically planned their work and worked their plan. How else do you become as iconic as those individuals?

Jay was a living testament to the fact that yes prison does trap your body but not your mind. Perhaps Recording Artist Jay-Z said it best on the album Reasonable Doubt. On a song called "Can I Live," Jay-Z says - "Lock my body, can't trap my mind;" Frequent conversations, all of which were no longer than 15 minutes, confirmed this for me. Through our conversations, he often appeared more hopeful than those whose freedom was not restricted. Not only was he hopeful, he was optimistic. Jay had dreams and goals. He had a plan for his life. He would share things with me in conversations and through letters attempting to troubleshoot his plans to avoid unnecessary challenges once released. Nineteen years served was more than enough time to master his game plan. Nineteen years behind bars was hard on me. I imagine they were even harder for him. Only the Strong Survived takes on a new meaning when you have a loved one behind bars. Correctional facilities across the country are filled with careless and hopeless individuals some of which will never see the day of light again. Imagine being around individuals or groups of people who no longer care whether they live or die. Now, imagine that you still care for your life and now have hopes and dreams as well as a loving and caring family to return home to. 19 years is long but it feels like an eternity when this is the case. Jay also had a daughter, her names Precious. I became an uncle at the age of eight.

Precious also known as Lou-Lou grew up a fatherless child like so many of today's young boys and girls. Jay would have to one day face this reality. Through our countless conversations we never ventured toward fatherhood. I was also young at the time so I understand why but even as I grew older it was not part of our dialogue. According to the Leadership Conference on Civil Rights (LCCR) one of every three black males born today will spend time in prison at some point in his life. Blacks make up 41 percent of the nation's 2.2 million prisoners. African Americans are incarcerated at nearly six (5.6) times the rate of whites while Hispanics are incarcerated at nearly double (1.8) the rate of whites. Externally Jay reflected the societal norms. He was a young, black, and male who chose a life of crime and would end up dead or in jail. He reflected the irresponsible African American Male who would not be present in his child's life thus allowing the cycle of crime and poverty to perpetuate. Although Lou' had a caring mother and a loving family, she still had a void in her life, she was without her biological father. I played my role as uncle the best I could but I was young and don't consider myself to have done the best job. It's hard. Prisons have managed to break-up homes and families. Slavery and prison have much in common. The effects run parallel to one another. Those fortunate enough to return to society often return home unable to read and write just as slaves did once freed. Many prisoners are hardened, unemployable and unable to market themselves because of appearance, perception and lack of skills. Very few return home rehabilitated. I see it all the time in my neighborhood. Within forty-eight hours of being released, many turn to the very thing that led them to prison in the first place. Jay was different.

Like many, Jay returned home vibrant, excited about life and his restored freedom. Guys in prison talked about their dreams and things they wanted to accomplish they were released. Many were seeking encouragement and grasping for hope. He was incarcerated in the early 90's so the new tech world we live in today was foreign to him. Like many who exit the prison system after a significant amount of time, Jay was institutionalized. His mind was free but his movements and thoughts reflected one who had been confined to the conditions of prison. Jay was aware of these traits. He experienced challenges once released and took some time to adjust but overall he was fine. Once released, he moved in with my mom. My mom prepared nineteen years for him to return home but was still not fully ready when he arrived. Like always, she made a way. She provided the basic necessities and helped him financially. Mom provided transportation to and from appointments. I provided clothes and a winter coat. I supplied him things he would need when meeting with potential employers and his parole officer. Image is everything. Luckily for me, the final three years of his time in prison he would send me the *Eastbay* Magazine with outfit's that reflected how he wanted to appear when he returned to society.

Everything he circled in the magazine was appropriate, clean-cut. It gave me an indication of how he wanted to present himself to the world once released. The things he circled were the types of things I purchased for him when he made it home.

Now home and free from the dangers of prison he rested. He was intrigued by the techy world we now lived in and wanted to get acclimated as quickly as possible. He started out with a cell phone. Those did not exist when he was last free. Learning to use the phone proved to be a difficult task but Jay is persistent. Texting, Facebook and social networking appeared as if it was something from out of space. Initially he was not intrigued, nor interested. His buddies would come over to visit. I think seeing his friends and basically everyone around him texting every second and constantly checking Facebook ignited a small interest. Technology had transcended the world he once knew. Slow to change he knew if he wanted to keep up he would have to eventually embrace where technology had taken us but right now he was not ready. In prison Jay became accustom to isolation. He required a lot of time to himself. His personal space had significant value to him. Jay was not in a rush to hangout, party or much of anything else. His focus centered around his place in today's society. His time alone, in isolation at my mother's apartment allowed him to do a test run on the plan he developed while in prison to determine if he had a legitimate shot at making it in today's world.

Jay met once or twice a month with his parole officer. He met regularly with Social Service Agencies the Prison Re-Entry program aligned him with. I think people look more closely at our actions during difficult times, when emotions run rampant and our guard is down but that's when our true character shows and we find out if our faith is real. Jay took pride in going to appointments and interacting with professionals. Curious as to how he would measure up as well as be perceived, he kept showing up. I often think part of him wanted to see how much his past would hinder his future but another part of him was determined to defy the odds. Jay showed up early and often. He was consistent. He was determined. Jay took full advantage of the services provided to former inmates. He learned to use the computer, he learned to search for jobs but most importantly he asked questions. Jay has never been easily discouraged. He is persistent in all that he does. He would look for employment, call employers and follow-up. Jay showed up every day. Workers began to take notice. Jay has a positive attitude and a will to succeed. Others were beginning to see that he was not your average inmate coming to the facility only to satisfy parole obligations. He was motivated and determine. He would come home and call me to inform me about his day. He would be excited with the amount of progress he was able to make each and every day. I was happy. I was happy because one, he is my brother. I was also happy because he was doing all the things we talked about the past nineteen years. He was living. He was determined to make a way for himself. I was happy because he was not letting pride or street cred or any other *nonfactor* get in his way. Jay had done what he said he was going to do. I have many friends in prison and nearly every one of them come home and do the very opposite of what they say. Jay honored his word. He felt good about the results but more importantly, he saw how important it was to get out and go after what he wanted.

Always intrigued with how he would measure up in today's world, he enrolled at Grand Rapids Community College (GRCC). While in prison he completed his G.E.D. Business and Accounting was his passion. Constantly pursuing excellence and striving for what many told him he would never be Jay was now a college student. More blessings were on the way. See, I am a believer that perseverance and hard work will be rewarded. From the time Jay returned home, he stayed consistent and committed to his plan. And even when things did not happen immediately for him he did not waiver or complain. Cascade Engineering would soon after, give my brother the opportunity that most convicted felons need, *employment*. Jay was gainfully employed, full benefits and health insurance. He rode a bike to work. His job was many miles away from the apartment. My mom worked during the hours he had to leave for work. This did not cause him to flinch. Jay would leave with enough time to make it to work an hour early. Once he obtained a car he would continue the same pattern. One day we were talking and he cut the conversation short to get ready for work. I said to him "Why are you leaving for work so early? You have a car now." He said; I like to leave early in case my car breaks down on the way, that way I'd have enough time to walk the rest of the way to make it on time.

Jay, within a year became Supervisor at Cascade Engineering. During that same time he began running his plant, bought a nice reliable car, opened up a savings account and secured his own apartment, furniture, cable, a laptop and internet. Jay is doing better than many who have never spent a day in prison. His transition into society has been seamless and he continues to thrive. At GRCC he made the Dean's List. He has been asked to speak at various professional functions. He was restored his relationship with his daughter and now plays an active role in her life and he has even found himself a girlfriend. Jay is living. I told him when his journey began to never let his past dictate his future. He successfully juggles his role as a son, brother, father, college student and professional and he does it staying true to the principles he believes will bring him success while making up for lost time. We talk regularly. Nothing has changed. I am happy he is home and we can talk for as long as we choose. We are no longer interrupted by an automated operator informing us that our call has one minute remaining. I am no longer subject to three hour weekend visits that seem to go by so fast. I can go over to his place whenever I choose, plus I have a key. He can come over and do the same.

IV   Chapter 4

A Winning Attitude

Your Attitude determines your Altitude

Don't be selfish; don't try to impress others. Be humble, thinking of others as better than yourselves. Don't look out only for your own interest, but take interest in others too.
Philippians 2:3-4

I hated every minute of training, but I said, "Don't quit. Suffer now and live the rest of your life as a champion."
MUHAMMAD ALI

How do you approach life?

I asked myself what my approach to life was and found out that it varied from day to day. My attitude however, was consistent. Learn how to be happy with what you have, while you pursue what you want. Learn to be content with who you are and where you are in life, but never settle. Strive for more. Learn to embrace the grind while enjoying the climb. Each day that I was blessed to see another day, I was thankful. I gave thanks to my Heavenly Father. Each extra day I was afforded to have on this earth I tried to make the most of it. Each day that my health was in good standing, I was also thankful. It wasn't until 2005 during and immediately after Hurricane Katrina that I realized this about myself and my approach to life. Prior to Hurricane Katrina, I believe I was on autopilot. I lived life just simply going through the motions. Prior to Hurricane Katrina, nothing that took place in or around my life, had neither a positive or negative effect. I was always kind of like, yeah, whatever.

Never let fear hold you back

Don't be afraid to fail. Be afraid of not trying. Too often I see people let fear hold them back. I see people let what others think of them hold them back. When you are already losing, you can't be afraid to fail. When you develop an attitude of quitting, you are sowing seeds of failure into your life. When you develop an attitude of not trying you sow a seed of mediocrity in your life. Choose to be great. Many others have chosen to be mediocre. It all starts with you. It all starts with your mindset. You must develop a championship mindset. You must develop a winner's mindset, a winner's attitude. We all have insecurities. We all have fears. In order to overcome them, we must learn to face them, not run away from them. I wanted to succeed too bad to let fear hold me back. I was too afraid of not trying therefore I had no time to worry about failing.

Championship Mindset

The Championship Mindset consists of these five things: Commitment, Accountability, Responsibility, Discipline and Faith. In order to develop a Championship Mindset you must be committed, accountable, responsible, discipline and have faith. You must possess all five of the characteristics in order to develop the Championship Mindset.

1. Commitment

> Commit to being committed. Stay true, consistent and committed to the things you want to accomplish.

2. Accountability

> Eliminate excuses out of your life. Eliminate distractions. If the people in your life are not pushing toward your goals, then they are holding you back and need to be removed from your life. But what is more important than the people in your life, is making sure you do what you say you are going to do.

3. Responsibility

> Hold yourself accountable for what you said you were going to do. Make sure others can depend on you but more importantly, make sure you can depend on yourself. Take responsibility for who you are and who you want to be. Stop blaming others. Blame you.

4. Discipline

> You get no days off from your purpose. You
> must learn to block out distractions in your
> life and remain focused on your goals. Never
> let anything knock you off your square.
> Maintain your discipline regardless of what
> is happening around you.

5. Faith

> Nothing is impossible if you believe. Faith is
> what makes dreams come true but you must
> work. Faith without works is dead.

Goals must be realistic and attainable

Shoot your shot, but understand what you are shooting towards ~ Chris Sain

One of the most essential things you need to do for yourself is to choose a goal that is important to you. Believe that you possess a basic goodness, which is the foundation for the greatness you can ultimately achieve. Goals are things you set out to do or accomplish. Your goals should be realistic and attainable. People will always ask and want to know what your goals are. People what to know what your purpose is. People want to know that you know what your purpose is and have a plan in place to achieve that purpose. Set the bar high but make sure your goals are reachable. Don't set yourself up for failure by establishing goals you know are unattainable. People set goals that are insurmountable then use their failure as an excuse. Small victories help build your confidence. Confidence improves your self-esteem.

Your goals should be visible at all times. They are your guide. I consider goals to be the blueprint and foundation for your legacy. Write them down. Develop a list of things you want to accomplish and tape it to the wall in your room or in the bathroom on the mirror. If you carry a journal, have your goals listed. Goals should be readily accessible. Your level of belief in yourself will inevitably manifest itself in whatever you do.

I wrote my goals down on a piece of notebook paper. Writing things down has always helped me store information in my head. I went to the school library and typed them out. I brought my goals home and placed three copies of them in the three rooms I spent the most time in my house. I put one copy in my room on the wall by the light. At night before I turned off the light, I took a quick look at my goals. I place a copy in the bathroom. Handsome people tend to spend a lot of time in the bathroom mirror. While I would get dressed, line my hair or brush my teeth, my goals were taped to the mirror. Even when I took a dump or got out the shower my goals were visible. Stop taking magazines to the restroom. Bring your goals with you to the toilet. Read and recite them until they become second nature. That's what I did.

Your goals should evolve although some may stay the same. Growing up my goals was simple;

1. Get up every day
2. Be productive every day
3. Look presentable.
4. Live every day as if it's my last.
5. Remain humble.
6. Treat people with respect.
7. Go to school.
8. Graduate from College.
9. Stay in my lane.

As you reach your goals, set new ones. That is how you grow and become a more powerful person.

I set nine attainable goals. Some will never change, others can be checked off. I leave room for adjustments because in life, things we pursue changes from year to year, sometimes month to month. As indecisive beings, we need to allow room for flexibility, change and uncertainties. To live life, it is best to enjoy what you are doing. Try not to spread yourself thin by trying to do too much. You may not accomplish every goal you set, no one does but what really matters is having goals and going after them wholeheartedly. One of my current goals is to work with professional athletes. To achieve that goal I needed to get more experienced working with high profile college athletes. I went out and became a mentor for student-athletes at The

University of Notre Dame. Success is a process that involves many steps. To achieve my ultimate goal I had to set preliminary goals. Knowing where you are going is the most important thing. How we get there takes time to figure out but having goals serves as your navigation system. Be determined to handle any challenge in a way that will make you grow. You are never too old to set another goal or to dream a new dream. Life has no limitations, except the ones you put on yourself.

Today my goals are broken down in sections; Spiritual, Personal, Professional, Family and Financial;

Spiritual Goals

Although I cannot remember the last time I went to church, I want to strengthen my relationship with the lord. I will read more of the "word" and continue to have faith in the lord.

Personal Goals

I want to save at least $3,500. I want to buy a new car. I want to speak on a more consistent basis in high school and colleges. I want to clean up my credit. I also want to be a better son, brother, uncle, friend and boyfriend.

Financial Goals

My goal for the year is to save $5,000.00 in my personal account. Realistically $3,500.00 for the year is more attainable. I will manage my funds the best way possible to reach my financial goal for 2010.

Professional Goals

I want to become the Player Development Director for a professional sports team. Form my own non-profit organization. I want to open up a Youth Center & Barber Shop to ensure a safe place for youth to build and enhance their self-esteem. Professionally I want to be a certified Substance Abuse Counselor. I want to dedicate more time to helping others and those in need. I want to speak on a more consistent basis at various schools. I hope to complete my "Supervision Hours" to become eligible to take my exam. I want to become a fully licensed Master Social Worker (LMSW).

Family Goals

My brother is now home from prison after nearly twenty years. I want to help build stronger family ties and relationships with both my mom and brother and overall family. I want to see our family become closer. I want the family to support one another on all levels.

Adolescence

I remember averaging 3 touchdowns per game in my first 4 games as a high school athlete.
I remember my name being broadcasted over the intercom every Monday for my Friday Night performances.
I remember making 11 tackles my junior year against East Grand Rapids.
I remember earning All-City Accolades as a Defensive Back in Football.
I remember being named the Ta-Wa-Si Invitational High School All-Star Basketball Game Most Valuable Player.
I remember competing in the Ta-Wa-Si All-Star Basketball Game.
I remember being selected to be on the Home-Coming Court.
I remember having girls at nearly every high school in Grand Rapids, Mich.
I remember visiting my oldest brother in prison.
I remember my favorite teacher - Mrs. Sturdivant.
I remember my least favorite teacher - Ms. Widdis.
I remember being voted most "handsome" my senior yr.
I remember going 2-7 my Senior Year in football.
I remember playing in the Holiday Christmas.

V   Chapter 5

Walk-On

Every Day is Game Day

Blessed is the man who perseveres under trial, because when he has stood the test, he will receive the crown of life that God has promised to those who love him.
    James 1:12

"Every day won't be a good day, but you can make every day ALRIGHT by the way you approach it!" ~ **Ray Lewis**

After graduating from high school it was now onto the next chapter of my life: College

The ACT and SAT is known as the college entrance exam and the one test that all students must take and that every serious, potential student-athlete must take and pass in order to be eligible for an athletic scholarship. Throughout high school I earned decent marks and was considered to be a model for student-athletes. I was embarking on a path that had not been traveled. Neither of my loving parents attended or graduated from college. Neither of my parents were college athletes therefore they were uneducated about the importance of the ACT. I guess I thought my talent alone and decent marks in school would earn me a scholarship. I was completely oblivious to the fact that my athletic future depended on the results of the ACT and without one I would have a much more difficult road ahead. I carried a 3.7 G.P.A. on average in school during my Junior and Senior year. Your Jr. and Sr. year were the years that many described as the most important if you want to get into college. I remember my low marks being a 3.3 or 3.4 G.P.A. Had I known about the ACT test and its importance, I would have studied and prepared for it to give myself a chance to earn a free education. Through hearsay I caught wind of a testing date to take the ACT. My best friend Carlton Brewster mentioned he was taking the test. During that time Carlton Brewster aka C.B. was Michigan's version of Donovan McNabb and Michael Vick. He had offers from Indiana, Michigan State, Northwestern and other elite college programs. The crazy thing about it was the testing site he was scheduled to take the test at, was at my high school. How could that be? Carlton mentioned to me how he was nervous and hoped he did well because he wanted his schooling paid for. It thought to my-self, I want the same thing. We're from the same neighborhood, the same humble beginnings. It might be a good idea to find out what time the test starts and what day it's on. In an unorganized fashion, I was able to get myself registered for the test date that Carlton had registered for. My level of preparedness was not where it needed to be at all. No study material but more importantly no knowledge of the implications of this test. For me, this was the last available test date. I did not know at the time that it was all or nothing. I thought I'd take this first ACT Exam to get a feel for what to expect. Often times I am able to master material once I am familiar with it. I completed the test and knew I did not pass but felt confident that if taken again I would do well. For other potential athletes, this was their third, fourth or fifth time taking the ACT Exam. Some took it more times than that. I have never been a good test taker. I knew my chances of passing the ACT Exam on the first attempt were unrealistic. In the history of my standard test taking career, I have never passed anything on the first try. The test started at 8a.m. and ended at 12p.m. Unprepared and uninformed, I submitted an exam that essentially made me a non-qualifier. Non-qualifier meant that I was not eligible to receive an athletic scholarship. Consider that strike one. During my senior season of football, I dislocated my left shoulder, my rotator cuff. Strike two. We finished the season with a 2-7 record. Strike three. I was devastated and overwhelmed as I transitioned from high school. I was entering college with the deck stacked against me. I had to prepare for the struggle of a lifetime.

Often times we, as African Americans, are uninformed about the necessary things in life. From teachers, to my parents and to my coaches, how could this important part of my future be overlooked? How could everyone drop the ball on the ACT Exam and its importance? For years I wondered why and constantly think about it to this day. Eventually I turned and pointed the finger at myself. I look at myself and blame me. No one else but me! It was a mistake that I would pay for my entire athletic career. It was a mistake that deprived me from the "Red Carpet" treatment scholarship athletes become accustom to. It forced me to walk-on to a program and lose reps to guys I was better than. But, think about it, I had no other choice. It forced me to pay college tuition at a university that was too pricey for my parents.

As a kid, I dominated rocket football also known as little league football, 78ers and high school sports. I knew early on in life that playing college football for the University of Michigan (U of M), the University of Miami aka the "U" or Florida State University (FSU) was what I was destined to do. I would later discover that God had different plans for my life. In the 90's each of those programs were extremely dominant. I would watch the games with my childhood friends and envision myself out there when I made it to college. Charles Woodson, Warrick Dunn, Peter Warrick and those types of guys reminded me of who I wanted to be. Then, life happened. Although a superb athlete, I did not have the type of career that would justify an athletic-scholarship to the University of Michigan or Florida State University. My high school team didn't win very many games to help gain that added exposure and notoriety. My junior year, which was by far the most fun I had, was made special by our transfer quarterback. By way of Ohio, A.J, who soon became like a brother to me, bonded on the sidelines of all places. We both went on to have a good year. My individual stats were mediocre at best my senior season on offense. The new offensive system we installed my junior year, was not a good fit senior year. The system did not complement my running ability or fully utilize my skill set. Post-secondary education was an afterthought. It was something that just was not discussed much. My high school coaches did not stress the importance of taking and passing the ACT. My coaches had access to limited resources, and they did not have relationships with major programs or coaches to vouch or advocate on my behalf or any athlete behalf. My head coach, Jerry Dutcher was a Michigan alumni and he knew the type player that was attractive to an elite program like Michigan and at the time only one player on our team fit the mold, his name was David Harris.

At the time I was somewhat arrogant, and thought I was better than what I probably was, looking back. I showed little to no interest in Division II schools and a chance at a free education because I thought I deserved to play on T.V. every Saturday. Division II Schools in the state of Michigan were schools such as; Grand

Valley State University, Ferris State University and Saginaw Valley State University to name a few. During my senior year of high school I considered Division II Schools as second-tier programs. I attended the Lloyd Carr Michigan camp with the likes of current NFL All-Pro Linebacker David Harris, currently with the New York Jets, Marlin Jackson, who later starred at Michigan and won a Super Bowl with the Indianapolis Colts and Ernest Shazor, two of Michigan's top recruit's in 2001. David Harris was my high school teammate. We have played ball together since Rocket League Football. At the Michigan Camp, Marlin Jackson, Ernest Shazor along with my-self was placed in the same Defensive-Backs group. I felt I held my own among those guys and that was all the confirmation I needed to know I could play at the Division I level. Marlin Jackson and Ernest Shazor were both noticeably bigger than I was. They were "Big 10 ready" at the camp. I needed to pack on a few pounds of muscle to justify playing corner in the Big 10 at only 5' 9". Looking back, I wish my parent's, a coach, or somebody would have stepped in, redirected my path and forced me to accept a free education. My life, good and bad forever changed with the choices I made.

I enrolled at Michigan State University (MSU). I believed all along I could play at the Division I level and besides, playing college ball was my dream from day one. I was away from home and it was my time to shine and take matters into my own hands. I thought to myself "This past summer I competed against the best from around the country." I had enough confidence remaining from my high school career despite our record as a team because of my performance at various football camps, including the Michigan Camp to play for the Spartans.

I arrived at the Duffy Daugherty Building ready to give it all I had to earn a spot on the MSU Football Team. Walk-on tryouts consisted of other athletes who dreamed of playing college ball while others hoped to make the team just to say they were part of something, believing it would give them status among their peers. I worked hard and did my best to display my skills and mental toughness. Tryouts were more mental than anything. Coach Mannie, MSU's Strength & Conditioning Coach facilitated the tryout. I caught his eye as well as the eye of other assistance helping out. As with anything, it's important to know how to transition from fitting in, to standing out. I made the cut. I most certainly made the team. Temporarily, I felt that I had overcome not passing my ACT and other obstacles I faced. Now, my mission was to earn a full ride athletic scholarship or take one from a scholarship athlete. For the moment I felt I had arrived and it was my time. To say I *played* college football at Michigan State University would be an overstatement. I practiced. I was most definitely a member of the team, but, I never attained a level of proficiency on the field that would justify a career at the professional level. Although I was an accomplished athlete coming out of high school, the reality of my situation was; I *walked-on* to the

Michigan State Football Team. I was surrounded by four (4) & five (5) Star Athletes, the Best of the Best. Critics use to say Michigan State was compiled of athletes who were not good enough to play at the University of Michigan. Of course as an athlete that statement sat in the back of our heads. We played and practiced with a chip on our shoulder and always strived to beat our so-called big brother. For me personally, those remarks really resonated with me. Michigan was where I wanted to play as a kid. I had to accept where my journey had taken me. Right now, that was MSU and I am now a Spartan.

Meanwhile, the Men's Basketball team had recently won the National Championship. Mateen Cleaves, Mo' Peterson and Charlie Bell headlined Michigan States 2000 National Championship team and Head Coach Tom Izzo was the hottest coach in the country. Football was a different story. Entering his 3rd season, Head Football Coach Bobby Williams was at the helm of a talented team on the field but off the field players lacked discipline and often brought negative publicity to the Football Program. T.J. Duckett and Herb Haygood went on to the NFL. When they left so did a lot leadership. The good news was that Charles Rogers and Jeff Smoker were returning. Charles aka *Chuck* was special. He was the best wide receiver in the country and arguably the fastest. Jeff Smoker was also special. He was the most efficient passer in the Big 10. Despite Chuck's God given talent and Smoker's efficiency, as a team, *inconsistent* best described MSU in 2002.

Success was not easily achieved.

In 2002 we lost badly to In-State Rival, Michigan (49-3) at the "Big House." That day I could feel it in the air. Something drastic was about to happen. Player morale was down, heads hanged low and critics were having a field day blasting our effort, and the coaching. Once we arrived to East Lansing, the team gathered at the Duffy Daugherty Building. It was quiet. An awkward silence filled the room. Coach Williams was fired shortly after the game. He addressed us and informed the entire team about his termination as Head Coach. Coach Williams had tears in his eyes. He packed up his office and talked about the most difficult thing with being fired is having to move his family. I was devastated and so were my teammates. I describe Coach Williams as a player's coach and looked at him like a father figure. It was at that moment that I realized the game I loved was no longer just a game. Wins and Losses had implications on people's livelihoods. Meanwhile, my life continued and although football was not going the best, on campus there was never a dull moment.

Known as a great party school to many, there was always something happening in East Lansing. My life continued to evolve. Socially life could not have been better. I met 10 unique guys from various parts of the country when arrived on campus and we called ourselves "The Circle." As a kid, people would say "there is no experience like college" and that in college "you will meet your life-long friends." Those statements are as true now as they were then. From Virginia to Connecticut all the way to Jackson and Detroit, Michigan we would form a bond that could not be broken. I once read a quote that said "best friends are the siblings, God forgot to give us." The Circle helped me take my mind off of all that was wrong with football. They were college kids, not athletes. They were just regular college students who planned to enjoy their college years and earn their degree along the way. They brought balance to my life. It is because of them I enjoyed the full college experience.

As a walk-on, every day was game day. After realizing there would not be much of an opportunity to play on Saturdays, practice became my Game Day. Learning to practice every day as if it were a game has done things for me that I never believed was possible. Imagine every day you step on the field is Game Day. Imagine what that does to you mentally. Being a walk-on helped build my character. Being a walk-on humbled me. Being a walk-on no longer mattered once my teammates noticed I had exceptional talent. To earn the respect of other players and your teammates sometimes is all that matters. I was a Defensive Back also known as DB. I played Cornerback which is commonly known as Corner, which meant I was responsible for defending the Wide Receiver and preventing him from catching the ball. As a member of the Scout Team also referred to as the Practice Squad, I would have the honor of defending the likes of Charles

Rogers on a daily basis. Because of the daily battles and resemblance we had, the two of us became good friends on and off the field. Many of the players and coaches thought we looked alike. They thought we were related. Coach Douglas, our defensive backs coach would always talk about staying on the divider, getting your head around, having good hips and making a play on the ball. He would often let the scholarship athletes know that one day I was going to take their scholarship. Being a walk-on was like being the low man on the totem pole. It's a step or two above being the ball boy or water boy. At Michigan State that also meant you got the early lift time with Coach Mannie.

My lift time was 6:00a.m Monday, Wednesday and Friday. Upperclassmen, Scholarship and Star Athletes had the option of lifting at a later and more favorable time. I remember plenty of days being pushed to the limit in the weight room. I remember throwing up and feeling nauseous. One morning after I finished my lift, showered and headed over to class, I realized that three times a week I go through the most excruciating workout and it has not broken me yet. It was at that moment when I believed *"what doesn't kill you makes you stronger."* Not only was I strong physically, I noticed how mentally tough I had become. My mental toughness has allowed me to endure many of life's challenges. Walking-on forced me to approach every practice like the actual game. Now, I approach every day of my life the same way. I put my game face on every day I wake and approach every single day as if it were Game Day. Imagine that!

Now day's I down play my athletic career to a large degree. Feeling like I did not have the career expected at the college level stifled my conversation. I find myself choosing to talk about others and their careers or other things in general. I think sometimes as athletes we can be too hard on ourselves but for whatever reason I shy away from the topic. I feel better when I am highlighting someone else's success or athletic career. I think it's a mechanism I use to keep the attention and conversation off of me and my career. It's funny how when I reflect on my past and consider my future, I'm doing better than more than half of athletes I know. But, when you pride your whole existence on making it professionally in sports, and fall short, it leaves a sour taste in your mouth. I remember telling all of my teachers and being so adamant about my future when they asked what I would do when I grew up. I answered Football or Basketball every time. When that did not become my reality, part of me felt like a failure.

One study indicated that professional athletes on average go bankrupt or have financial difficulties three to seven years after their playing days are over. I guess being a walk-on taught me to prepare for a rainy day. Rainy days were all too familiar to me. I learned the best way to deal with the rain was to have a good umbrella. Long ago it was said that "Life isn't about waiting for the storm to pass…It's about learning to dance in the rain." Working hard is all I know. Nothing ever came easy. Nothing was ever handed to me. I wasn't born on 3rd base; I stepped to the plate and hit a triple. I walked on at MSU, earned a spot on the team, I went to class and showed up every day. I was never provided a silver spoon, nor did I benefit from white privilege. Nothing was ever handed to me. Everything I have accomplished and obtained, I've earned it. I went out and took it. I didn't benefit from having known someone. I could not call someone up and ask for a job. These things have shaped my perspective, my character and my principles. This is part of why I feel I can accomplish anything. I am blessed. I am only twenty-four years old. God has truly blessed me and I know without a shadow of a doubt he favors me.

Nothing came easy

As long as I can remember, I have had to earn everything. I believe handouts lead to complacency. I believe that when you earn something or when you work for something, you appreciate it and cherish it more. When I made the team, it meant something to me, because despite what anyone had to say, I could say, I earned it. Easy Street is the road most people take which makes taking short cuts ok. Easy Street allows you to become dependent on others. See, all I know is hard work and all I know is that nine times out of ten, I won't be out worked.

Growing up in the inner-city, again, I did not benefit from a silver spoon or white privilege. I witnessed early on how easy things came for others and how hard I had to work. I often wondered why things were this way. In school, some students never had to study while some refused to study and they would still earn a better grade than me even with my hours of study. The one thing I hated was when others acted as if they believed they were going to fail a test because it was a way for them to come down to your level only to ace the test, then say "I thought I was going to bomb this test, I didn't study at all." I remember as a kid, talking with my white friends in school and it amazed me that at an early age they knew the college they planned to attend as well as what they would major in. What was more amazing was that in addition to the college, they also knew there tuition was already paid for. An academic scholarship or grant they were awarded was extra money for them to do nothing with. Wow! Here I am on the other end of the spectrum rushing home every day after school to go to the park to work on my game so I could have a shot at earning an athletic scholarship to college. Why is that, I thought? How can a kid that is 12 years old already have is schooling paid for? What does his parent's know that my parents don't know I began to ask? How come our lights, gas and cable is frequently turned off? These types of questions represented just a few of the things I asked myself along the way.

It's something about college that helps you transition into adulthood. I believe that knowing mom and dad is not there to wake you up for school, or buy you shoes or clothes does something mentally. For me, I felt it helped me become more independent. I remember coming home and my parents being blown away with how responsible I had become. Despite these things, nothing came easy. As a walk-on, I still had to find ways to pay my tuition. Classes at MSU are expensive. I often felt dumb for not doing the responsible thing and going to school for free. I was the first person in my family to go to college. I think the thought of me being the first to earn a degree blinded my parents to the financial strain I was causing. Filling out forms such as FAFSA for federal student financial aid was foreign to me and my family. My parents would struggle to make ends meet trying to pay for my schooling. I felt as if I was yet another expense for a middle class family already faced with plenty of bills and cut-off notices. The pressure was building. Every day at practice, I felt the need to make a play in order to standout, in hopes of earning a *full-ride (athletic)* scholarship. My reps were few and most of my time was spent on the scout team. I thought to myself one day, how am I going to earn a scholarship on scout team? How much longer can I continue to be a financial burden on my parents? Again, these were the types of questions I was faced with day in and day out. I thought to myself, was I a dumb athlete making more dumb decisions? Or, am I selfish and unwilling to accept that my dream of playing college ball will have my family living on the streets?

Nothing came easy. My math class was getting extremely harder as the semester progressed. After morning workouts which pushed me as close to death as one can imagine, making it to class was becoming extremely hard. Sore and drained from workouts, I stumbled into class only to find the remaining open seats in the nosebleed section of the class. I couldn't keep up. My coaches assigned me a tutor, and that didn't make a bit of difference. It was obvious that math was not my thing. For me, nothing came easy. I was faced with a very difficult decision. I had to either drop this 5 credit math class to preserve my G.P.A. and risk falling under 12 credit's and becoming ineligible, or remain in the class, receive an F for my final grade in a 5 credit math class which ultimately destroys my G.P.A. and brings me below a 2.0 G.P.A. I had a huge decision to make. The implications of my decision could ultimately affect my status on the team, alter my dream and eliminate any chance of earning a scholarship to take the pressure off of my parents. In my mind, I struggled with the little voice in my head. The little voice reminded me that failing this class would confirm that I am a dumb athlete and being ineligible to play would be the proof. Now 18 or 19 years old, the dumb athlete perception is still following me and right now, has a good chance of proving itself right.

I chose to stick it out. I chose to fight. I chose to remain in the class and try my very best. I even went to my professor's office hours, something I was not accustomed with, in order to gain sympathy, because for me, nothing came easy. None of that worked. I earned a 0.8 which is the equivalent of a F. My G.P.A. was shattered. What's next I asked myself? Trying to be proactive, I tried to retake the math class at Lansing Community College (LCC). As my luck would have it, they did not offer a 5 credit math class. I was caught in a jam. I also believed at the time that Junior Colleges also known as Community Colleges were easier than universities. Hindsight is 20/20 but boy was I wrong. My reality now looked like this; I am a walk-on who just failed a 5 credit math class which destroyed my G.P.A. Already expendable, I lost what leverage I had and it truly was over. See, for me, nothing came easy. I wondered why me? Why were things always so difficult in my life? How come I can never catch a break? Nothing came easy and these are the questions that I asked myself. Maybe it is true. Maybe I am a dumb athlete and that is why nothing came easy. I wanted to make excuses. I wanted to blame everybody else for my struggles. It was hard for me to look at myself, my habits and my actions…but I had to.

To my credit these trials served as my motivation. They say "only the strong survive." Obviously I was still alive and the fact that I was alive and my health was intact, I was determined to do something about my situation. If you are not dead, you are not done. In life, it's not about what happens to you but how you respond to what happens to you and although nothing has ever came easy, I've learned to appreciate the struggle. I began to troubleshoot all things I might encounter and develop a contingency plan for the unexpected. I wanted to do all I could to minimize my challenges. Historically nothing came easy so I made sure I prepared. I developed a plan for my life. I created a backup plan to assist with the unforeseen and the unexpected. I had to change my fortunes. If you fail to plan, then you plan to fail. I was tired of the struggle and refused to be defeated by things I could control. As a walk-on student-athlete, it taught me the importance of planning and preparation. My career was never certain. My life as football player had no consistency. As a walk-on, nothing came easy. I learned I had to be built to last but more importantly built to survive and persevere. It wasn't easy, but it was worth it!

Side Show

Can you work when nobody celebrates you? It's not about you! That was the biggest lesson I learned while playing college football. For the first time in my life, I was an afterthought. For me, that was a huge pill to swallow. Now, it was up to me to figure out how I could contribute to a cause greater than myself. Can you work when nobody celebrates you? Can you work when it is not about you? That is what I had to ask myself. It was not until later that I was able to honestly answer that question. But who knew learning to work, in a way that enhances the life of others would one day pay off in such a major way for me. I transitioned from a selfish person to a selfless person.

Humbled

On one end I was completely satisfied with walking on to the MSU football team, besides I earned it, but on the other end, the fact that I was a walk-on always remained in my subconscious mind. For me, the preferential treatment the scholarship athletes received was what I yearned for. An athletic scholarship served as a reminder that the university had a vested interest in you as a student and as an athlete. The university was willing to pay for your education in exchange for your athletic gifts. Although I had offers, I was not offered an athletic scholarship by MSU. There was no contractual agreement in place and nothing binding me to the university or the university to me. Making the team was indeed a huge accomplishment, but yet caused insecurities to creep into my mind. See, some of us are never satisfied. I should be happy and on cloud 9, instead I felt incomplete.

As a competitive person, I too believed I deserved preferential treatment. I earned it. It's what all the hard work was intended for coming up as a kid. Less superior athletes attended the university on full-ride scholarships and it was frustrating to know that while I'm struggling to pay my college tuition, there are guys that have it made. Back at home, my family was struggling to make ends meet. At school I was struggling to make the grade and barely felt part of the team. Not because of anything MSU or my teammates did, but because of my own mindset about being a walk-on. These thoughts represented my subconscious mindset. In reality, my teammates were like family. Not one member of the team ever made reference to the fact I wasn't on scholarship. I can't vouch for what they did when I was not around. Still, I was humbled by the reality of my situation.

Being a walk-on is now part of my story. I minimized conversations about my time at MSU for the sake of knowing that as a member of the football team, I was not on a full ride athletic scholarship. I watched them on T.V. each Saturday and cheer for them. I bleed Green & White. My time as a walk-on was life changing. The experience was invaluable and my teammates are forever family. We had a chant that signifies our bond. After every break down we would say "Spartan Dawg's 4 Life." We all bleed Green & White. Every year football season comes back around I am faced with the same insecurities all over again. Chris? Didn't you go to State? Didn't you play ball at State? What year? What position did you play? Who was the coach at the time? Each and every year it's the same thing. I have all of my answers to those questions memorized now. I have even learned to prepare myself for all other questions related to State. I attend Homecoming Games and always enjoy connecting with former Spartans. Each year I get better with dealing with the fact I was a walk-on and I have learned to embrace my journey.

I have been humbled. Humility has become my best friend. I've learned that if you live long enough, life has its way of humbling you. I knew God but had not yet engaged him. I left Grand Rapids, Michigan, young, arrogant, and confident. Some would replace confident with cocky but it's all a matter of opinion. With no scholarship, a failed math class and no money to pay tuition, that arrogance and confidence was replaced with shame and embarrassment. My reality forced me to take a deep look into myself, my purpose and my circumstances and once I looked in the mirror it was apparent that I could not go on this way. My spirit was humbled. At the time, I still possessed a great deal of self-confidence but I presented with a much softer approach, and became sensitive towards the hardships of others and their struggles. My conscious is clear. I can now walk around, head held high and confident about where I've been, where I have come from and where I am going.

VI   Chapter 6
<u>School Boy</u>

Big Man on Campus

Wisdom and money can get you almost anything, but only wisdom can save your life.
Ecclesiates 7:12

"Now Street Guys stand in College Admission lines thinking it's cool to get an Education."

#Influence

While at Michigan State, I was nowhere near the star player on the football team. The last time I was the star of any team, was in high school. However, I was a star on campus and in the dorms. From the day I stepped foot onto the MSU campus I knew college was for me. At my disposal, I was enrolled with, at the time, over 44,000 students from all across the world. At eighteen years of age, I felt like I was in heaven. I've always had a way about myself and a way with the ladies. Michigan State just gave me a bigger platform to do what I was best at. I entered college with a girlfriend. My high school sweetheart went to school at Tennessee State University (TSU), a historically black college that was many miles away from East Lansing,

Michigan.

We often talked on the phone but I soon realized that long distance relationships were not for me. I felt in order to enjoy the full college experience I needed to be free. I needed to be single. Meanwhile, the guys at TSU were taking notice of my high school sweetheart and like most women, they love the attention. We would argue over missed phone calls, suspicion of the unknown and lack of trust. I would hear guys in the background along with loud music when I would call. She would say they were at a sports bar with a group of friends, girls and guys, hanging out having a good time. We were upfront and honest about most things. She told me she was into another guy. That gave me the out I needed to terrorize MSU entire campus, the graduate and undergraduate students.

We would keep in touch and hangout when we returned to Grand Rapids for Christmas and Spring breaks but it wasn't the same. We were growing apart. She was really into the down south appeal and I was enjoying the thousands of women who were in love with me. Looking back, it all worked out for the better. I was finally single. I wanted to enjoy the single life and its benefits but a really good friend was waiting in the wing. She would come up to MSU from Grand Rapids, Mich. to visit. She would bring various items to fill up my mini fridge in my dorm room. We became really close. I guess when you are a college athlete it's easy to get attached to someone who is there for you, during good and bad times. She was always there and she was always supportive.

I had plenty of female friends, but none mattered the way she did. I would return home on the weekends or during away games when I did not dress. I would end up staying with her the entire weekend barely seeing my own family. She had become my family. Her family looked out for me. They did not live anywhere near the hood' so I always thought her spot was a good escape. I hated to come home or go to the barber shop. The reason why is because everyone in my city asked one question and one question only, and that is "are you starting." My home town was so accustom to me being the dominant athlete that they assumed I would have the same success at the college level. I prided myself on keeping it real, so I gave the same lame answer every time "I'm doing my thing in practice, but you know how it is." I hated not being able to provide a better answer.

My girlfriend, who is a couple years younger than me, would later enroll at Eastern Michigan University (EMU). Eastern is located on the "east" side of the state. We were from the "west" side of the state. She was pretty. Many said she looked like J. Lo. It wouldn't be long before the Detroit guys took notice. Detroit guys are different from Grand Rapids guys. Knowing where she'd come from, I knew the stylish, flamboyant Detroit Playa would be enticing. Sure enough, I started getting that vibe like things were not right. I tried to beat her to the punch. I called and told her:

"I don't want to deprive you from the ultimate college experience. I've had my experiences and you deserve to have your own. If a guy wants to take you out or to a movie, you should not have to think about a boyfriend in that instance, you should be able to go. Spread your wings. I want you to spread your wings and enjoy the college experience."

Looking back I was too nonchalant. I practically gave my girl away. She was young, a couple years younger than me. They say "If she's yours let her go. If she comes back, she was meant to be. If she doesn't, then she never was." She never came back. We hung out during Christmas & Spring Breaks but the east side of the state had a much bigger influence on her at the time then I did. I often think about my choice of words on that phone call. I often replay that conversation in my head. I go back and forth about did I do the right thing or not. Whether I did or not, I had to learn how to live with regrets. I had to move on. It was back to my playboy ways. I was on the market and unwilling to get involved in another serious or committed relationship.

Back on campus, I hit up every party and ran through all the dorms in the "Brody." My thinking while at MSU: "Any man can sweep any woman, off of her feet, if he has the right broom," right? I had the right broom. My buddies also notice how easily I attracted the ladies. I never wore my Michigan State

Football Apparel. I never wanted the girls to associate me with football. If you liked me, you liked me for me, not for what I do. I always kept it that way. Some females never knew I played ball, some didn't care. To be well rounded meant more to me than being the guy who played football.

Every now-and-then I took advantage of being a Spartan. I would ride with star wide receiver Charles Rogers to parties or teammate Robert Flagg, a good friend at the time who was from Florida and when the football team was in the building we got the red carpet treatment. Flagg had that '03 Impala on 20's. I felt good riding around with him. I just stood close to those guys and did what they did and before I knew it I had a drink in my hand and was in the club for free. The one thing I loved about Michigan State and my teammates was the fact they were all down to earth people. We all had good times together, on and off the field.

Many people desire to be the "Man" on campus. For me, staying in my own lane was most important. The college experience is one I will always remember. Depending on who you talk to, they'll tell you how they were this or that. Jay-Z said it best: "No matter where you go you are what you are…" I realized in college that for whatever reason I got along well with others. I made friends easily, and was a person that many called on to help them through their problems. The same love and admiration I received in high school, I received in college. The difference, it was ten times more than what it was from high school. Being out on your own, away from family will help make you a man. Any person can call themselves the "Big Man on Campus" but what really matters is the man you become when you leave campus.

The Circle

The Circle consisted of ten guys but the core seven had the biggest impact on my life. Franklin Smith better known as Franky or Nitty, Kerrhon Kelso better known as Kelso, Day Lee better known as V.A., Jesus Castillo better known as Manny, Xavier Martin better known as Zay, Eric Dickason better known as C.R.E.A.M., Gary Jones better known as Gary and Jermaine Buchanan better known as Hood.

Many people say College is where some people meet their life-long friends. I was blessed to meet a group of guys that would not only help shape my life, but help me out more than they would ever know. Coming from my city, the inner-city and the perceptions that were put out there by others, I did not know cool guys went to college. Sadly, when you are from the inner-city or the hood, the only example of college we had were the depictions made on television and movies. Me personally, I thought that college kids all resembled Carlton from The Fresh Prince of Bel Air. I was completely shocked when I arrived on campus and entered the dorms at Michigan State University (MSU).

Each member of the Circle brought their own unique personality to the group and to the campus. Franky, from Jackson, Michigan, not only was an exceptional student in the classroom, but was socially just as popular and had a way with the ladies. I can honestly say that the ladies had a thing for him as well. Franky carried himself well, dressed nice, coupled with the perfect blend of intellect and humor. Very mature for a freshman, as our friendship grew, I would soon find out that his mother died when he was around a sophomore or junior in high school. When he shared that with me, it was kind of devastating in a way. For me, I was raised by both of my parents and couldn't imagine losing either of my parents. To see how resilient he was and how positive he was said a lot about his character. Frank was very ambitious. He let it be known during our freshmen year that he would one day have a Lamborghini. That's Franky. He always set the bar high for himself and others and was willing to go after what he wanted out of life. Despite losing his mom, I know she would be very proud of the man he became. He earned his bachelor's degree and graduated from Michigan State University in 2005.

Jermaine Buchanan, or as we call him *Hood*, also from Jackson, Michigan was Franky's best friend. He fit in perfectly with the Circle. Jermaine dressed nice. To be honest, I have never seen him without a haircut. Hood had a baby girl while in college and his daughter was his everything. Hood's demeanor was a bit more laid back than the rest of the guys but he knew how to have fun with the best of them and had a great sense of humor. Not only could he give out jokes, he could take them as well. The thing I loved about Jermaine was that, he never took himself too seriously. Throughout college it was joy to watch the friendships we all had with each other but none greater than the friendship Franky and Jermaine shared. They were more like brothers, with Jermaine being the older brother. He also earned his bachelor's degree from Michigan State University.

Kerrhon Kelso but known to many as K. Kelso or Killa hails from Flint, Michigan. Thank God for Kerrhon. Because of Kerrhon we had no excuses to be late for class or parties. He was a time freak. Thanks to Kerrhon we were fashionably late but still on time. He would end pre-game, which is known to college students as the drinking we do prior to going to parties, assign a Designated Driver (DD) and make sure we were everywhere on time. Kerrhon wore his thoughts on his sleeves. He had no problem saying what was on his mind. He could make you laugh and embarrass you in the same sentence. Probably better than any other members of The Circle, Kerrhon balanced his social life and academics, equally giving time to both. Before exams I would always ask him was he ready and he would always reply with *"I'm ready as I am going to be, I've studied so whatever I don't know by now, wasn't meant for me to know. Oh well."* That is a typical response from Kerrhon. What you see is what you get. He was one of my best friends on campus and one of my favorite people. Every member of The Circle was very overprotective of Kerrhon. He was the voice of reason of the group with great organizational and time management skills. We were never late to class or a party and Kerrhon is the sole reason why. He also earned his bachelor's degree from Michigan State University.

Eric Dickason but known on campus as C.R.E.A.M. is from Detroit, Michigan. By far the funniest of the group he was just as exceptional in the classroom. C.R.E.A.M. spent most of his college career making fun of Jermaine and repping Dip-Set. Monday through Sunday, 24 hours a day C.R.E.A.M. would make jokes about Jermaine and others but primarily Jermaine. In another life, Eric would have had a successful career as a comedian and actor. He was very talented, very funny. What I liked about Eric is that he stood out from what was considered the norm for guys from Detroit. He ran the girls wild and they loved him just as much but honestly I think he could care less about any of that. Eric just wanted to have a good time. He was always the life of the party, the Brody, and the cafeteria. He was fearless. We could put him up to do some of the stupidest things and C.R.E.A.M. would gladly accept. Eric earned his bachelor's degree from Michigan State University.

Gary Jones, from Benton Harbor, Michigan was one of the better athletes in the group. Gary loved God and he loved basketball. The impressive thing about Gary was that he came from a city that many would agree, lacks hope and everything about Gary represented hope. Gary carried himself as if he was somebody. Gary had a purpose. He was going somewhere with his life. Gary was also very competitive. He had a winners spirit. Some may downplay it, but Gary was funny. He could tell jokes with the best of them. He had an infectious laugh and bottom lip that we always made fun of. A handsome guy in his own right, he had good hair, he was not vertically challenged and enjoyed having fun with his close friends and family.

David Norfleet but known on campus as V.A. came to us from Portsmouth, Virginia. VA brought a southern swagger to the crew. His country accent combined with his east coast and southern swag quickly became a household name on campus. Like other members of The Circle, VA had a great personality; he was very funny and enjoyed having a good time. Always up on the latest fashion, VA had a shoe fetish. He kept the hard-to-get pair of sneakers, Retro Jordan's, boots and anything else you can name. VA also holds the crown for being the life of the party, the dorms and cafeteria. Some people just possess that infectious personality and VA simply had it. He earned his bachelor's degree from Michigan State University.

Jesus Castillo but known to us as Manny, hails from Boston, Connecticut. Manny and his Boston dialect was one of many unique features he possessed. A die-hard Red Sox fan, we would always rep Boston regardless of how many Michigan, Tigers, Red Wings or Lions fans were present. The Red Sox, New England Patriots, Celtics and any other sports team from Boston was Manny's favorite, Just like CREAM and VA, Manny was the life of the party, loved hip-hop, Fat Joe and East Coast music. Like the rest of the group, Manny knew how to have a good time, loved to hang-out, laugh, joke, laugh at CREAM joking on Jermaine and party. I think out of all people, everyone loved Manny, I have never met anyone who did not have love for Manny. It was just something about him. He was cool. He was real. He was chill. He was laid back. He was Manny. He also earned his bachelor's degree from Michigan State University.

Xzavier Martin but known as Zay, is from Detroit, Michigan. Not only were we teammates, we were roommates. Zay was the total package. He was funny, crazy, the life of the party, dorms and Brody cafeteria. The stories with Zay are endless. He was very athletic, very good in football and basketball. He was very good in the video game "Madden" football and loved to gamble. Zay played football at MSU and like the rest of the crew worked at the Physical Plant also known as the Phys. or the Phys. Plant. Zay never missed an opportunity to make some extra money on the side. Zay would put money up against anybody in the dorms when it came to Madden on the PS2 and did not care if it made him late for work or put his employment status in jeopardy. Zay loved the city of Detroit and repped it to the fullest. Zay made sure the entire crew experienced memorable moments together. With Zay, there was never a dull moment. He was turnt up before the phrase became popular. Zay was the oldest out the crew. He was the big brother and the little brother all-in-one. Zay, despite being the oldest and taking the longest to graduate out of all us, eventually graduated and he too earned his bachelor's degree from Michigan State University.

In many regards, the members of the Circle meant more to me than the members of the football team. They helped me find a balance in my life, showed me how to live life and have fun and most importantly they took my mind away from all that was wrong with football. They remained true and nonjudgmental, yet supportive and encouraging. Unlike my teammates, we did not compete with one another, we just simply had fun and enjoyed the college experience, partying and doing crazy stuff most of the time.

The beginning of the end of my football career

While away at school, my mom and dad's marriage was falling apart. Growing up they flirted with the idea that once Preston, my little brother and I were out of the house, they would get a divorce. As a kid I thought arguments between parents consisted of remarks like that. I never paid much attention to it. I was however, always aware of how unhealthy their marriage was. My mom had a tendency to hide issues that we were going through as a family. I remember visiting every prison in the state of Michigan and while talking with Jay, my oldest brother who was serving nineteen years at the time, she would make things seem ok at home. She would do whatever it took to make my brother believe that the marriage was fine or that everything was good at home.

Often times my mom and dad argued over the smallest of things. Every Sunday before church, I remember the two of them arguing. Every holiday, I remember the two of them arguing. It became routine. If they made it Monday through Saturday on good terms, I could pretty much bet that would all change by Sunday morning. Many people have misconceptions about two parent households and assume that things are always better. Away at school, I was removed from the everyday struggles my family was faced with. My mom would call up to my dorm and we would talk. I would ask her how things were going at home and she would always assure me that things were fine and that there is nothing for me to worry about. Due to the fact I was living the college life, that answer brought assurance and I didn't think twice about life back at home. One day that all changed.

My mom called and I could sense that something was wrong by the tone in her voice. See, my mom has a very sweet and soft voice and although at the time she would not say, I could tell something was not right. I began to remember how many family problems we hid from my brother Jay and thought to myself, my family could be withholding things from me. Why wouldn't they. I'm away at school, trying to be the first child in the family to bring home a college degree. It made sense. Sure enough that was the case. I took a more vested interest in the happenings of my family although I was away. I soon found out that my mom and dad were on the brink of divorce, another woman was involved, and his business was crumbling. My little brother was also having issues and now flirting with the streets. It was complete madness back home. I understood why my mom kept those things away from me, but I did not accept it. I felt she should have informed me of all the chaos involving them as opposed to trying to hide, deny and cover things up.

Family problems have a way of affecting the mind, body and spirit, then couple that with the demands of being a college student, playing football and dealing with injuries, it begins to feel as if you are carrying a ton on your shoulders. Football was always a means to do more for my family. Now more than ever my family needed me and football was not panning out. I began to stress. I started to panic. I felt I had to do something to help my family. I flirted with the idea of giving up football to get a job. I had no work experience and outside of football, gave very little thought to what I would do next. I felt stuck. My back was against the wall and I did not know what to do. I was at a crossroad. It came down to family or football. Football was supposed to help out the family and the family was supposed to support my football career. Everything was in disarray. The reality of my situation was; I am a walk-on, who most likely has a very little chance of ever playing. My shoulder is damaged and due to my parents situation they don't have medical insurance therefore my shoulder will never fully recover. Back home the family is going through some tough times, they need me and I need them.

I returned home and now I was amongst the madness. I was physically present to see just how bad things really were. I was disappointed. I was torn. I told myself I could not let my dreams go to pass because of this foolishness. See, when you are away, things sound and seem terrible but when you are able to see things for yourself, it allows you to determine for yourself whether these are self-inflicted problems or genuine family concerns. I knew in my head I would not be home long. I saw the traps that so many in our community succumb to. I was determined to not fall victim. As much as we love family, it is family that sometimes hinders your success or blessings.

Pit-stop: Grand Rapids Community College

I enrolled at Grand Rapids Community College (GRCC) where I played one year of football before transferring to Saginaw Valley State University (SVSU) to pursue my dreams of playing ball on a football scholarship. I had not had much success to that point as a college athlete. The GRCC stop was intended to help me restore my confidence. I needed to see for myself was I as good as advertised. I needed to see what it felt like to play and have a significant role as part of a team. If nothing else, GRCC helped me accomplish that. I had the chance to meet and play with guys such as Pacino Horne who would later star at Central Michigan University, Brandon Walker who would later transfer to Hampton, Eric Malloy, Tamayrr Salahuddin who later starred at Grand Valley State University, Juanta Phillips, Ed, D. Copes, Tim King, Chris Lovelady, Dennis Doe, Tyrone Spencer, Billy Bob and Bo Bo, Sleezy, Ron Jackson and Carlos Robinson who participated on the practice squad for the New Orleans Saints to name a few. They were hungry. They wanted to get to where I had been. They helped me get that edge back.

Last Chance: Saginaw Valley State University

In 2004, my dad transported me to University Center, Michigan. Saginaw Valley State University had a little money to pay for my final two years of eligibility. I figured I would finish my last two years at SVSU and do well at my pro day to at least be picked up as a free agent by an NFL team. My thought was, as a Division I caliber athlete with NFL potential, I would dominate the Great Lakes Intercollegiate Athletic Conference (GLIAC) more commonly known as Division II and have enough body of work (film) to justify a career at the next level. That was definitely not the case. I suffered a dislocated rotator cuff while at GRCC and because my parents were going through their mess, I did not have medical insurance therefore I was unable to get my shoulder the medical attention it needed. This was an injury that I was more than familiar with. This time it was my right shoulder. I originally suffered a dislocated rotator cuff on my left shoulder in high school that haunted me throughout my college career. My left shoulder was surgically repaired while I was at MSU. My range of motion never returned. I felt like I spent more time in the training room than on the field. I was devastated and could not figure out why this was happening to me. I felt my coaches started to believe I was injury prone. Doubt began to creep in, and I started to believe I was injury prone. My mental state was being challenged. It was beginning to be too much but if I am going to call myself a Christian, I have to honor Jesus during the disappointments too. As a team we had a lot of success. We were well respected in the GLIAC. Todd Herremans currently with the Philadelphia Eagles led the way on our offensive line. Ruevell Martin and Glenn Martinez who respectively played with the Green Bay Packers, Denver Broncos and Houston Texans were Wide Receivers. John DiGorgio, our defensive leader and All-American Middle Linebacker played with the Buffalo Bills. There was other NFL potential on our roster as well. We maintained an extremely competitive environment thanks to the likes of Sheldon "Hog" Cantrell, Chad Steele, Michael Crawford, Corey Gonzales, Jeff Mackey, Dan Fodrocy, Ric Cottengim, Stan, Bobby Awrey, Alex Voltaire, Joe Johnson, Logan

Barnhardt, Matt Black, Michael McClenny, Mark Miller, Brent Rogers, Bobby Belmonte, Mark Radlinski, Derek Volmering, Doc (the twins), Jermaine Jackson, Lenny Dantine, Solo Brittain, Stephenol Santos (Boo), Luck & Neil Baumgartner, T.Scott, Vinnie Miroth, Carlos Swoope, Marion Steward, DePhil Coleman, Robert Smith, Edmund McAllister, Damien DeRosia, Nick Lillie, Brandon Emeott, Edric Prim, Tony Alessi, Justin Mays and Josh Miller. We challenged each other every day.

Football never materialized. Things did not go the way I envisioned they would. Success seemed light years away and it had been a long time since I had any. The dream I had for myself was fading. The one thing I knew I was certain of at the time was that, I would not return home. I didn't care what the reason was; I just knew going home was not an option. I remember calling my dad, writing my brother who was in prison at the time and talking with my mom. I remember telling them that it was over and time to move on. It was time to hang up my cleats. See, I've played football since I was 8 years old. Football has been part of my life for 16 years. It was the most difficult decision I have ever made. I was walking away from the game I loved but the game no longer seemed to love me back. The love was gone. The pain, the setbacks, the injuries and the politics took its toll. Add the fact that I had not experienced any recent success as an athlete and it became too much. I was searching. I searched high and low for answers. I entered school as a student-athlete. I was no longer an athlete. I focused my efforts on the only thing remaining, my education. I have always felt that God remains in control despite the situations we find ourselves in. I believed he would use my situation for his Glory. I never doubted if God was watching over me. I reminded myself he sent his son Jesus to make a way out of no way. Football was supposed to allow me to touch lives. Seeking refuge while sitting alone in my room, I was reminded that God wants us to touch lives wherever he leads us. I had to find a new passion.

In the midst of it all, God made a way. Despite all the things that occurred in my life up to that point, I could now look back and say for the first time in my life, football was not the most important thing to me. The phone calls to my family were difficult but at the same time a weight was lifted. I began to realize that how I lived on earth was just as important as my salvation. Football didn't work out but God has me here for a reason. It was up to me to figure that out. When I first arrived to SVSU another Division I player had transferred in. His name was Delando Bradford. He was a Freshman All-American at the University at Buffalo that transferred to be closer to Sherise, his girlfriend. Delando was a Christian Athlete who believed strongly in the word of God. Our paths made us close mainly because we were both Division I athletes now playing Division II football. We would soon become roommates and two of the best cornerbacks in all of college football, so we believed. Commonalities and similar interest made us instant friends. Instantly you could see Delando's talent. He was a hard worker with an excellent work ethic. It was obvious why he was a Freshman All-American plus he had that it-factor coupled with God's favor. I thought I was a hard worker until I met him.

Iron sharpens Iron. Delando and I complimented each other in many ways. Our styles as defensive backs were different, but our mentality's were the same. We were both aggressive corners that didn't mind helping with run support and that could make a play on the ball. As sure tacklers and cover corners, we shared the same vision. We both believed that God had led us to SVSU to fulfill our dreams of becoming professional athletes. The fact that we both had Division 1 experience, we believed that playing at the Division II level would add value to our stock at our pro day. As college roommates I was able to see another side of Delando. He went hard on the football field, but he went even harder for the Lord. He was constantly in his word. He prayed. He leaned on the Lord during difficult times and he stayed in worship. As a man of God myself, Delando was much further along in his walk with the Lord than I was at the time. I knew the Lord, but had not yet engaged him although he was still guiding my path.

As friends off the field Delando and I grew stronger in the Lord. The trials and tribulations we both experienced as college athletes had strengthened our relationship. Looking back, I believe it was divine that

Delando and I crossed paths and ended up at SVSU. See, sometimes God places individuals in your life to convey his message. I started to realize the Lord will do multiple things with your life and not to bank on just one thing. This is something I now understand! At the time I was banking on football to make all things right. My true purpose and passion was starting to reveal itself. Delando transferred from Buffalo to be closer to Sherise. Sherise and Delando dated. They were a beautiful couple that was spiritually connected with the Lord. Sherise attended Eastern Michigan University, located in Ypsilanti, Michigan. She was a singer. Sherise was part of a gospel group out of Detroit. She grew up in the church. I was able to see firsthand how to make a long distance relationship work. She would visit on the weekends and during the season she would come up on Game Day. At times you could see the commute and the distance taking its toll on their relationship but their faith in God and each other helped them pull through. For me to see another athlete living righteously and refraining from drinking, smoking, partying, fornication and other lascivious behaviors was a first, but was also impressive. Delando showed me that there was another level I had to elevate my life to. A spiritual level! Day-in and day-out he demonstrated how to balance his responsibilities while never compromising his relationship with the Lord.

In 2007 Delando and Sherise got married. I was asked to be in the wedding. Their union was special. Delando would also graduate with his Bachelor Degree.

The favor over his life looked real good. At the time I wasn't quite where he was in my personal life but the way he was being moved toward things by the spirit was something to see. For the both of us, football had come to an end. With his degree in hand, he returned home to Detroit, Michigan a married man. I completed my Bachelor Degree and headed to graduate school in Detroit. What happened between Delando and I was divine. God blessed me with a teammate, roommate, a Brother in Christ and I even participated in his wedding. We have had numerous long talks about many facets of life. Delando is still happily married and now serves our country as a U.S. Marine.

Looking for Love

Witnessing Delando's relationship and eventual marriage is what made me think about what I wanted in my partner. During my time at MSU I met hundreds of beautiful women. I had a "Top 5" list of women that featured attributes I wanted in my wife or at least someone I could be serious and settle down with. When I first arrived to campus in 2001 I met Corinthia Wilson also known as Queat at the end of the first semester just as we were leaving for Christmas Break. It was something about her I remember telling myself. I couldn't wait for the break to be over. I was very much interested in getting to know Queat a little better. Franky, my best friend at MSU went to high school with Queat and had a little background information he was able to provide me with. He told me that she had a son and that he watched him from time to time while she worked or attended class. He agreed to introduce me. We became really good friends over the years. When I transferred our communication kinda fell off a bit but every now-and-then she would cross my mind. Years had passed. I noticed I remembered her phone number by heart. In a world that has everything stored in a phone now-a-days, to remember a number by heart says something. It says a lot. Now at SVSU, camp was approaching for the upcoming 2004 football season. I decided to make one last trip to MSU prior to camp to see Queat. Very family oriented she had her nieces over. Between her son and her nieces, it was tough to get very much accomplished. Plans I had for us during my last trip were quickly set aside. I chalked it up as a loss and enjoyed the kids. Watching her interact with the kids was a sight to see. She was amazing. Parenting came natural. A year later and now back in Saginaw, I found myself thinking about her again. This time when I checked in, it was around December and she was headed to see her family in New Jersey. Thinking about how far the two of us had come, I could do nothing but thank my man Franky for orchestrating this from jump. Miles apart, I decided to send her a letter;

Love Note

As you prepare to go away in search of what may be your next big move in life, take the time to reflect on special people in your life. I have told you before about my feelings, but regardless of how I feel, your feelings are what matter most. It's hard to feel a certain way about someone when you don't know what they feel. Despite what your feelings might be, no matter what, they matter to me.

If I told you that I wish you were my girl, you probably would feel pressured or unsure about the situation. If I shared my vision with you of seeing us together, I might get let down because you might not share the same vision. Some days I swear it gets hard. Some days I wonder if I even deserve someone like you...

Only God knows what the future holds, and who knows, you might meet the man you deserve, right there in New Jersey/Philly. So, me being me, I definitely don't want to be a burden in that sense. My thing is I hate to see you single, and I always joke around with you not ever having anyone, but that might be for a reason. When I look at myself, I don't have anyone either. Ironic, but true, that's the way it is.

If for some reason you get lucky, and you find someone, very special, who treats you right, I will be the first to tell you how happy I am for you, but if you don't maybe you should consider me as a possible candidate. Who knows...you might be the reason I

begin to eat right, and go on to live to I am 101 years old.
Anyway, this is from me to you. Just a little something to think about on your flight...Remember I love you and I mean this when I say it. Have fun and enjoy yourself. ~ Chris.

I'm coming home

I returned home with a Master's Degree. I was a first generation college student and graduate. I brought a Master's Degree back home. The inner-city could now say with confidence we had degrees in the hood. I was proud to bring degrees back home to my neighborhood. My new mission now was to inspire others to do the same. I hoped my bachelor's and Master's Degree inspired my peers to return to school or finish school. I hoped the young kids in the neighborhood believed graduating from college was possible. I strived to make sure having a degree looked cool. *Cool* is what most of today's youth respond to. A college kid with swagger was unheard of. I had swagger, local celebrity, superstar status, clothes and cars, all things that matter to the youth in today's generation. Prior to my return home, college was for geeks and nerds. Inner-city youth often have a false perception of what type of individuals comprise of a college campuses but they knew I was neither, so I was able to dispel that notion.

Not everyone was convinced. See, often when you try to do better for yourself jealousy and envy presents itself. The adversary will always try to attack your purpose. His mission is to kill, steal and destroy. Those back home who was not inspired took shots at what was otherwise a historical accomplishment. When out in public or at local nightclubs, I would often hear the whispers. People would say *"he's Hollywood now that he has a degree"* or *"he ain't nothing but a college boy."* At first I took offense to people's comments. I use to think to myself, "when did I become *Hollywood* or I'm not a college boy, I went to school because I was an athlete." Then, one day it dawned on me. I sat and thought about the kind of people who were making those comments. Most did not go off to school. Most were ones who chose a different path. I began to see opportunities to change that perception with the understanding that college is not for everyone but it is for some, and it was for me.

I found that when I would talk to those that felt that way, by the end of our conversation there perception had changed. I learned that it is natural for humans to feel indifferent about things and people based on choices. I chose college. I began to embrace the *School Boy* title. I embraced it in a way that it became cool to be called or considered a school boy. Education is key for success in today's world despite what the ignorant or uneducated says. I capitalized off the emergence of online education and nontraditional students returning to school to gain new skills or obtain their degree to advance within the company. Going back to school or enrolling in a community college became the new phenomenon. To be in school was cool. To say you were going back to school was cool. The title School Boy took on a life of its own. I earned my advanced degrees at a young age. I now look at how many I've inspired to go to school. I look at how many of the ones that once called me *Hollywood or College Boy* are now enrolled or considering college. That's the power of Influence.

VII   Chapter 7

Book Smart | Street Smart | Common Sense

The Importance of Education

For it is by grace you have been saved, through faith – and this is not from yourselves, it is the gift of God – not by works, so that no one can boast. For we are God's workmanship, created in Christ Jesus to do good works, which God prepared in advance for us to do.
Ephesians 2:8-10

"90% of Failures come from people who have a habit of making excuses"

Today "there are over 400,000 college athletes and almost all of them will turn "Pro" in something other than sports." This mantra is true. Think about it. Take a moment to think about athletes who were exceptional, then ask yourself, where are they now? Controlling your own destiny is the key. In life, as well as sports you will have experiences that you cannot control. Unforeseen events, injuries, accidents and tragedies can alter the course of your life. It is important to control your own destiny.

I was a star in high school but when I went to college that was not the case. In college, the stage is bigger, the stakes were higher and politics, alumni and money became more of a factor. Livelihoods are on the lines, rival game outcomes could lead to coaches being fired or having your coaching contract extended. Athletic Scholarships are limited. Scholarship Athletes are the investment, no matter what, they play. Everyone likes a return on their investment but what's sad is many athletes fail to get anything out of the deal. They may receive money, cars or other gifts from boosters, agents and coaches but many bypass the biggest gift of them all: Education. Many athletes leave early for the pros or are dismissed by the program for being in violation of the Student-Athlete Code of Conduct. Others have conduct detrimental to the team or consistently violate team rules. Politics and lack of loyalty causes the rest to transfer to other schools and programs where there is chance and opportunity.

While in class, at practice or in my dorm room, I sat and thought about life. I always thought about what if things don't go my way? What if this is not my calling? What will I do? This level of deep thought caused me to look at things differently. See, in football, there is a small window of opportunity to have a successful career at the professional level. The allure of money, inadequate life skills, limited organizational skills and poor time management skills negatively affect the average athlete. Coaching styles and changes, systems, ownership, management styles, injuries and personal problems plague the athlete as well. These factors give most athletes a small window of opportunity to succeed and experience longevity as a professional athlete.

For me it was important to be in control of my life. On my wall in my room read a quote: "God, grant me the Serenity to accept the things I cannot change, Courage to change the things I can, and Wisdom to know the difference." – Serenity Prayer.

I realized I could not control how things went with football. Will I start, will I play, will I travel or will I get injured. I learned to accept that I could not control those things. What I could control was how I performed in the classroom. I chose to study; I chose to read the chapters. I chose to complete my assignments on time and attend office hours to form personal relationships with my professors. I chose to earn my degree and achieve academic excellence in the classroom. At an early age, I had the wisdom to know the difference. I began to make decisions accordingly.

Today my life is simple. I approach every situation with a keen sense of what I cannot change. I scan the same situation, and determine the things I can change. I've always trusted my gut and my instincts. My professional discretion and intuition has rarely led me astray. Once I took life by the horns and started to control my own destiny, I was able to earn my bachelor's and Master's degree by the age of twenty-four. Being young-black and educated made me an anomaly in the professional world. Having the credentials opened doors and provided opportunities that otherwise would not have been available to me. I was a Dangerous Black Negro.

Education proved to be much more valuable to the overall quality of my life. I have something to fall back on while I pursue my other dreams and aspirations. In a predominately white man's world, education levels the playing field. Respect is easier to establish. Most importantly they look to me as the expert. I take my story everywhere I go to hopefully inspire at least one person. A quality education allows you to control your own destiny. The same effort it takes to be the best athlete is required in order to be the best student. If you approach both the same, the reward is priceless.

I have positioned myself to be successful, but even more so, to impact others. Influence means more to me than power. I am thankful for those I have mentored and influenced. I also try to be an example to others outside of my circle. It is important for the young to see how prosperous life can be if you stay in line. I believe at the end of the day, we all want the same thing, and that is to live a quality life. To achieve that life you have to do the things that allow you to control your destiny. Many people today allow juvenile and correctional facilities to control their life. When you are allowed one hour a day outside or when you are told when to eat or get up, is not considered living. I want to make sure today's youth understand there are alternative ways to live.

Going to school and earning a degree is not the only way to control your destiny. The key to controlling your destiny is living righteous, and making an honest living. Treat others the way you want to be treated and help those that you can. Life is not complicated. Sometimes we complicate life. Taking care of your community and those in your community affords you a promising life. Everything you do for others will come back to you in abundance. The bible teaches us to be anxious for nothing. What is for you is for you. You will get yours. We will all get what we desire. You have to go through whatever it is you will go through to arrive at your purpose.

Golden Ticket

Education is the key to your Liberation

College is not for everyone, but, it was most certainly for me. I encourage you to at least take an interest in a trade if you believe college is not for you. Times have changed. You need credentials, certifications or a degree to advance in today's world. Stories like Bill Gates very rarely exist in the hood. My dad, although a very successful entrepreneur, I watched him go through the back door instead of the front. Eventually he accomplished his purpose and reached his goal but I thought to myself, there has to be a better way to advance then going through the back door. When I was a child he told me that a college degree was mandatory. He said that high school was a prerequisite and there was no need for discussion whether I was going to obtain my high school diploma or not. My dad believed that I could avoid some of the barriers he faced by getting a college education. He was always ahead of new trends. He told me early on that a college degree would open many doors and that it would provide endless opportunities.

First Generation College Student

Typically, a first generation college student means that neither of your parents has earned a bachelor's degree. A first generation college student refers to the fact that you are the first person in your immediate family to attend college. That was me. I was the first. College always appeared to be a place that was not accessible to Urban African American Males. Very few college guys existed in my neighborhood. In fact, I did not know of anyone who attended college or aspired to go to college. To be honest, the only reason why I attended was because I had to in order to play college football.

Being the first in your family to go to college sounds good when you are talking with your advisor or girls you're trying to impress on campus, but the reality of being a first generation college student is scary. For one, you have no point of reference. Secondly, no one in your family can tell you or show you how to be a successful college student. It's not like being taught to ride a bike before removing the training wheels as a kid. The most difficult thing of all about being a first generation college student is that typically for the first time you are away from home, away from your parents and you're at a place where no one looks like you. No one shares your experience, so it seems. These three factors are often why most minority students return home after the first semester. Some never return, due to carrying around a belief that college is not for them.

Find People on Campus who Support You

One factor that changes the college experience is finding someone you connect with on campus. That person could be an advisor, your counselor, someone in admissions or the enrollment center. Learn about the various student organizations on campus. Find those on campus that are looking to support you.

The unfortunate thing about getting support on college campuses is that the support does not standout. Colleges do a poor job of pairing and assigning minority staff to first generation students. Often times a minority student is directed to the "right person" by someone other than who they have assigned and designated for the actual job. For many, it is often too late by the time minority, First Generation College Students find the *right person*. Colleges are filled with people that somehow, whether intentionally or unintentionally taint the college experience. The football program at MSU had a built-in support system.

Although many were not a good fit, at least they were solely out for the best interest of the student-athlete. I transferred to Saginaw Valley State University (SVSU) and had a completely different experience. There I met Calvin McFarland and Tony Thomson. Tony was a white guy that worked in the counseling office for first year students. Although I was not a first year student, I connected with Tony while in search of an internship. While interning for him, it turned out to be the best college experience I had. Tony was the first faculty member at any college to show compassion toward me. He took a liking to me and it was obvious it was genuine. He was kindhearted and very passionate about people, about his job and about his family. His interest in me changed my entire college experience and the perception I had about college. He saw and tapped into potential I didn't know I had. He helped me discover my gifts', he helped me discover my purpose while in undergrad. I credit his compassion toward me for fast-tracking my success upon graduating and entering the adult world.

Calvin was a favorite for every SVSU student. He was a middle aged African American male faculty. He was rare. He was a director and held a leadership position of a respected office at the college. It was refreshing to see one of us in leadership and with power and influence. Calvin simply got it. You could tell after five minutes of conversing with him that his experiences growing up rivaled what mine were. That simply meant he could relate and truly understand challenges I was faced with as an urban minority college student. Calvin wore his leadership hat and his *"get-on-your-level"* hat well. He was always professional but yet real and relatable. He is what every campus needs to help minority students and First Generation Students transition to college and the college experience. Thank God for Calvin and the role he played in my college success.

Access Campus Resources

College Campus Resources usually include advising, counseling, personal counseling, disability support services, student organizations, tutoring, career planning, academic related workshops and financial aid among others. Student orientations are often designed to get acclimated with the available resources on campus. The experience is similar to a drive-by or an assembly line at a factory. A drive-by consists of a brief introduction to the different departments and resources on campus. Unfortunately, they are very rarely done in a fashion that connects with First Generation College students. I remember going thru the drive-thru aka orientation and connecting with nobody. The process seemed superficial. No one was really real or made you feel like they hoped to see you when classes started. This disconnect is to the detriment of minority students across the country.

The best academic resource I came across while I was in school was the library. Taking the time to learn the areas in which I was not as strong and learning how to discipline myself, show some restraint with my newfound independence and setting aside adequate time to study and master the course material. The library served as a quiet peaceful place that was generally located a good enough distance away from my dorm. Something about the library atmosphere helped me focus. It seemed that the other students that were present in the library were focused and serious about their academics.

College is nothing more than a game of chess. Once you figure out how to be a successful college student, manage your party and social life and utilize resources and office hours, it's really not all that bad. Set short-term realistic goals such as making it from semester-to-semester, completing papers and assignments outlined in the syllabi, waking up and attending class consistently. And before you know it, adapting to the college culture feels routine.

Figure out your learning style and how to balance your time

The quickest way to find success in school is discovering your learning style. No one style fit me. Figure out what way you learn best. For me, I knew I responded best to the real life application of course content, which is also why I majored in social work, I preferred classroom instruction with a teacher present versus online learning. I needed to know how I would use what I was learning in real-life. Along the way I discovered I was not a natural talker / speaker although I could conjugate verbs, articulate well and speak thoughtfully. My greatest strength was my written communication skills and my ability to communicate and articulate my thoughts on paper through writing. This skill would prove to take me far as a college student.

Just as important as figuring out your learning style is learning how to effectively manage your time. Time management is crucial to being a successful student. I broke my day down in 8's. We all have twenty-four (24) hours in a day. What you do with your 24 determines how successful you will be.

$$\{8+8+8 = 24\}$$

I learned that I didn't need the full eight (8) hours of sleep if I ate right and went to bed at a decent time. I learned that I could function perfectly fine off of four (4) to six (6) hours of sleep. So I began to use my 24 like this 4+4+8+8=24. I learned that I was the sharpest and most alert in the morning. I was a much more productive student during the morning classes than I was during my afternoon and evening classes. This discovery led me to selecting earlier classes. This increased my chances of earning better grades because I was more alert, sharp and productive in the morning. This little bit of insight into my-self and who I was as a student paid huge dividends.

#Success Tip: Figure out your learning style and how to appropriately manage your time.

The Seven Learning Styles

- <u>**Visual**</u> **(spatial):** You prefer using pictures, images, and spatial understanding.

- <u>**Aural**</u> **(auditory-musical):** You prefer using sound and music.

- <u>**Verbal**</u> **(linguistic):** You prefer using words, both in speech and writing.

- <u>**Physical**</u> **(kinesthetic):** You prefer using your body, hands and sense of touch.

- <u>**Logical**</u> **(mathematical):** You prefer using logic, reasoning and systems.

- <u>**Social**</u> **(interpersonal):** You prefer to learn in groups or with other people.

- <u>**Solitary**</u> **(intrapersonal):** You prefer to work alone and use self-study.

Using sports as a platform will transcend the way we interact with youth.

I remember returning home from college during Christmas Break in 2003 and looking around my neighborhood only to see not much was going on. Nothing within the community targeted our youth. Nothing catered toward their interest. I would spend time with family and friends as we shared thoughts about the college experience, but in my head I knew something was missing. The youth had no voice or positive outlets. They had very few pro-social activities to actively engage in and there seemed as if there were even fewer positive role models.

I returned to campus in East Lansing but could not seem to stop thinking about youth back home with little to look forward to. After I would complete my class work, I would brainstorm ideas and different ways I could return home and make a difference.

As always, I shared my vision with my little brother, Preston and my best friends Carlton Brewster and Eric Malloy. They to agreed, no one our age was doing anything for our youth. All of us were under twenty-five years old at the time. We decided it was up to us to lead the way and show our community and peers the way. Leaning on our superstar appeal from days when we were high school standout students and athletes, we used our local celebrity and influence to influence others. Co-founded by Preston and I, I developed the vision for Grand C.I.T.Y. also known as Grand C.I.T.Y. Sports, Inc. and how to proceed. With donations from members of the organization and my own money we created Grand C.I.T.Y. Together we carried out and delivered on the things we thought were missing in our community.

During the Bush Administration we experienced some tough times. None tougher than what we experienced in urban communities though! President Bush finally acknowledged that our country was in a recession. In my home town, families were struggling. Adults we grew up looking-up to, were losing their jobs and homes. Times were hard. I witnessed good, hardworking people in the city hit rock bottom, including my family. My best friend, Carlton Brewster aka C.B. suggested we provide turkeys for as many families as we could. It sounded like a great idea. When you have a servant's heart, you are always looking for ways to bless others. We chose New Faith Temple Church, which was his dad's church. We asked our parents for money or whatever they could spare as well as Gordon Food Services. Neither was able to provide much. We took what we collectively had and brought turkeys. That year, November 2008, we provided 112 turkeys to deserving families in the Grand Rapids area. That year we embarked on something that was more meaningful than anything we had accomplished in our athletic careers. We learned and seen first-hand the power of giving back. That was our 1st Annual Turkey-Give-a-Way.

I believe that giving back builds character. I also believe that with a small dedicated group, there is nothing that can't be accomplished. Grand C.I.T.Y. is a community driven non-profit organization Committed to Influencing Today's Youth (C.I.T.Y.). We believe in community outreach and feels it gives us the chance to not only teach, but show youth how to be productive young adults.

Tony Robbins said "Life is a gift, and it gives us the privilege, opportunity, and responsibility to give something back by becoming more." This reflects the philosophy of Grand C.I.T.Y. During our 2nd Annual Turkey Give-a-Way, we provided 384 turkeys to deserving families and we set a goal to bless 500 families in the following years. All of this was in addition to speaking engagements, annual football camps, basketball camps and other events.

Working with people, especially youth and young adults is my passion. Youth today need so much more, they need various types of role models and people who care about them and that are willing to show and teach them the way. I decided that I would step up to the plate, be someone youth across the world could connect with, relate to and identify with. This commitment came with a cost, a cost that needed to reflect the time I committed to put myself in position to inspire and influence others.

VIII   Chapter 8

Non-Qualifier

Temporary Setbacks prepares you for an awesome Comeback

Be anxious for nothing, but in everything by prayer and supplication, with thanksgiving, let your request be made known to God.
Philippians 4:6

Life is about balance and avoiding burnout. Smile about the little things, laugh at your imperfections. I do. That's a winning formula

I was bound to fail before I had the chance to succeed. It's what I called a double-whammy. My biggest fear had found a way to derail my future. The one label I feared most was now attached to my hip. Only a dumb athlete would experience what was about to happen next.

I was not eligible to receive an Athletic Scholarship because of my low ACT score. I was a Non-Qualifier. A Non-Qualifier is a college-bound student-athlete, who cannot receive athletic aid also known as scholarship, cannot practice and cannot compete in the first year of enrollment. My low ACT score left me with no other option but to walk-on. In order to play collegiate sports, a student-athlete must be a full-time student. This means that a student-athlete must be enrolled in 12 or more credit hours. If at any point a student-athlete drops below 12 credits that student-athlete is deemed ineligible. Yes, I am an expert on this info now. However at the time I wasn't. I was playing ball, I was enrolled in 12 credits and considered to be a full-time student when all of a sudden things got real in my math class. A first generation college student and unaware of what to do in the situation, I dropped the math course to save my G.P.A. Unaware of the ramifications dropping the course would have on my eligibility coupled with the fact that as a walk-on, I didn't have immediate access to the support services scholarship athletes did. At the time, this felt like a major setback for someone who was already expendable. To be honest it was a major setback.

Temporary Setbacks often referred to as challenges or obstacles we face in our lives and is another way to phrase and look at things that happen to you. So, next time you experience something that did not go your way, consider it a temporary setback and know that you are only preparing for an awesome comeback.

Examples of things I would call Temporary Setbacks would be: Failing a Test, Quiz, Mid-term or Final Exam, Getting Injured, Breaking up with your girl/boyfriend, Losing your job, Transferring Schools,

Giving up a big play during a critical stage of the game, Making a mistake, Losing, Failing a class, Ineligibility, Fighting/Anger Outburst, Letting someone or something get to you, Testing Positive for Substances, Being Criticized for something you did wrong.

Learning to accept failure and criticism says as much about a person as anything else. Learning how to accept failure is important because failure can lead to poor decisions which can alter the course of one's life. It is important to understand that we are all fallible. We all make mistakes and fail at something. But, what is more important is how you respond to what happens. How you respond to things that happen to you says a lot about your character and the type of person you are.

In middle school during my 8th grade year, I was the star player on the Junior High Basketball Team. I looked forward to basketball season because I had just finished a really good 78ers football season. The first game was days away when I found out that I did not have a 2.0 GPA. I was devastated. This meant I would not be playing ball my final year of Middle School. At the time, I let Iroquois Middle School down as well as my coach and my teammates. This temporary setback prepared me for an awesome comeback. When I got to Ottawa Hills High School, I dominated as a freshman in both football and basketball in 1997 and never looked back. Individually I had a successful high school career. I received numerous accolades and various awards.

In college I struggled in math. There were at least 150 students in my lecture-styled math class and I had trouble learning the concepts. No matter how early I arrived to class, the only seats available were in the very back. I sat so high up and far away, the professor looked like an ant. I sat in the nosebleed section of the class. Sometimes I could barely hear what he was saying. By the end of the semester I had a 1.2 GPA in that class. I was unable to comprehend, learn or keep up. Failing that class wrecked my GPA. That class was worth 5 credits. After failing that class, I retook the class at a nearby community college. There were thirty students in this class compared to 150. After restoring my GPA, I went on to become an Academic All-American.

If you view all the things that happen to you, both good and bad, as opportunities, then you operate out of a higher level of consciousness. My temporary setbacks led to very strong comebacks. My approach to adversity and my commitment toward excellence along with my faith in God made all things possible. I have had plenty of experiences that caused me to bounce back or pick myself up. As humans we all do it every day. Coming back from challenges faced or problems in our lives is what makes each person special and unique.

The setbacks, challenges and obstacles that I've faced has challenged my mental toughness. It is because of life experiences that I know that no matter what, I can come out on top. My faith in God and my understanding of the fact that he will never give us more than we can handle helps me to believe, even during times of despair. Because of my understanding of "everything happens for a reason" I have learned to accept the good and the bad and make the best out of both situations. My glass is half full therefore my outlook on life is filled with hope. I have learned to find the good in every situation. Most importantly I have learned that temporary setbacks are part of life but how you comeback makes it all worth it.

Just My Luck

A two-decade-long battle to stop the National Collegiate Athletic Association (NCAA) from relying on racially biased and educationally unjustified SAT and ACT cutoff scores to determine who can participate in interscholastic sports and receive scholarships has finally come to an end. Unlike me, student-athletes entering college in summer 2003 and thereafter, an eligibility formula combining high school grade point average and test scores will replace arbitrary minimum test score requirements of 820 on the SAT or a combined score of 68 on the four-part ACT. This is huge, especially for urban student-athletes attending public schools who otherwise lack access to college. It was just my luck that I entered college the summer of 2001. In high school I carried a 3.3 Cumulative G.P.A but had a low ACT score. Had I earned the same marks and entered college two years later, I would have been what is known as a Qualifier and perhaps my career would have taken a different path. Instead I was what you called a Non-qualifier, a label no athlete wants to be associated with.

The new "sliding scale" will allow student-athletes who demonstrate strong classroom performance in high school to offset low ACT or SAT test scores. For students with grade point averages midway between A and B on the standard marking scale, only the lowest possible SAT or ACT score — obtainable simply by filling in the bubbles on answer sheets randomly or even leaving every item blank — will be necessary. Enrollees with high school grade point averages of B- (2.75) or better will also face significantly lower test score hurdles than in the past (see chart). For those with lower grades, SAT/ACT requirements are unchanged.

The NCAA policy change, which was approved by the association's Board of Directors, represents a major victory for minority coaches, civil rights activists, and test reformers. Over the years, FairTest has played a central role in this effort. Unfortunately for me this policy change was two years later. But thankfully for student-athletes coming after me their athletic aspirations won't be derailed by a racially unjust test.

**New NCAA
Initial Eligibility Index**
(effective August 2003)

Core Course GPA	SAT M	ACT Combined
3.55 or higher	400	37
3.50	420	39
3.25	520	46
3.00	620	52
2.75	720	59
2.50	820	68
2.25	920	77
2.00	010	86

Source: NCAA Initial Eligibility Clearinghouse

Information changes Situations

My people are destroyed for a lack of knowledge ~
Hosea 4:6

The Initial-Eligibility Standards for NCAA Division I College-Bound Student-Athletes Are Changing

College-bound student-athletes first entering an NCAA Division I college or university on or after August 1, 2016, will need to meet new academic rules in order to receive athletic aid (scholarship), practice or compete during their first year. Don't be like me. Learn from my mistakes. Be better than me.

What are the New Requirements?

Full Qualifier	Academic Redshirt	Non Qualifier
Complete 16 Core Courses: • 10 of the 16 core courses must be complete before 7th semester (senior year) of high school. •7 of the 10 core courses must be in English, Math, or Science.	Complete 16 core courses.	Does not meet requirements for Full Qualifier or Academic Redshirt s
Minimum Core-Course GPA of 2.3	Minimum Core-Course GPA of 2.0	
Meet the Competition sliding scale requirement of GPA and ACT/SAT score.*	Meet the Academic Redshirt sliding scale requirement of GPA and ACT/SAT score.*	

Graduate from high school.	Graduate from high school.	

NCAA Eligibility Center - (Clearing House)

Athletes that plan on competing at the NCAA Division I or Division II level are required to register with the NCAA Eligibility Center (formerly referred to as the NCAA Clearinghouse). The Eligibility Center evaluates your amateur status, core courses taken in high school, GPA, and standardized test scores to determine if you're eligible at the Division I or Division II level as a freshman.

Remember, you cannot participate in Division I or Division II athletics if you aren't cleared by the NCAA Eligibility Center.

Registering with the NCAA Eligibility Center

Online registration takes less than one hour at the NCAA Eligibility Center website. Detailed information about registration is available online and by downloading the NCAA's Guide for the College-Bound Student-Athlete. Ideally, you should register during the summer after your junior year of high school.

Divisions I and II Initial-Eligibility Requirements

NCAA Divisions I and II require 16 core courses. See the charts below.

Beginning August 1, 2016, NCAA Division I will require 10 core courses to be completed prior to the seventh semester (seven of the 10 must be a combination of English, math or natural or physical science that meet the distribution requirements below). These 10 courses become "locked in" at the start of the seventh semester and cannot be retaken for grade improvement.

Beginning August 1, 2016, it will be possible for a Division I college-bound student-athlete to still receive athletics aid and the ability to practice with the team if he or she fails to meet the 10 course requirement, but would not be able to compete.

Meeting Core Course Requirements

Core courses are academic courses taught at a college preparatory level. If you are not sure if some of your classes meet these criteria, ask your guidance counselor.

Core Course Requirements for Division I

- *4 years of English
- *3 years of math (Algebra 1 or higher)
- *2 years of natural or physical science

- *1 + year of English, math, or natural science

- *2 years of social science

- *4 years of extra core course (any category above or foreign language, comparative religion/philosophy)

Core Course Requirements for Division II

- *3 years of English

- *2 years of math (Algebra 1 or higher)

- *2 years of natural or physical science

- *3 extra years of English, math, or natural or physical science

- *2 years of social science

- *4 years of extra core course (any category above or foreign language, comparative religion/philosophy)

Standardized Test Scores/Grade Point Average

Division I uses' a sliding scale to match SAT and ACT scores with a core grade-point average. A minimum GPA of 2.000 is required in your core courses.

Division II requires a minimum SAT score of 820 or an ACT sum score of 68. A minimum GPA of 2.000 is required in your core courses.

Note: When you register for the SAT or ACT, use the NCAA Eligibility Center code of 9999 to ensure all SAT and ACT scores are reported directly to the NCAA Eligibility Center from the testing agency. Test scores that appear on transcripts will not be used.

Amateurism

NCAA eligibility rules also require amateurism certification. The NCAA Eligibility Center asks several questions about your participation in athletics to verify your status as an amateur. Some items that may raise a red flag concerning your amateur status:

·   -A contract with professional team

·   -Prize money or salary earned through athletics

·   -Tryouts, practice or competition with a professional Team

·   -Benefit's from an agent or agreement to be represented by an agent

·   -Delayed full-time college enrollment in order to participate in organized sports

·   -Any financial assistance stemming from athletic participation

Grade-Point Average

Be sure to look at your high school's List of NCAA Courses on the NCAA Eligibility Center's website (www.eligibilitycenter.org). Only courses that appear on your school's List of NCAA Courses will be used in the calculation of the core GPA. Use the list as a guide.

Division I students enrolling full time before August 1, 2016, should use Sliding Scale A to determine eligibility to receive athletics aid, practice and competition during the first year.

Division I GPA required to receive athletics aid and practice on or after August 1, 2016, is 2.000-2.299 (corresponding test-score requirements are listed on Sliding Scale B on Page No. 2 of this sheet).

Division I GPA required to be eligible for competition on or after August 1, 2016, is 2.300 (corresponding test-score requirements are listed on Sliding Scale B on Page No. 2 of this sheet).

The Division II core GPA requirement is a minimum of 2.000.

Remember, the NCAA GPA is calculated using NCAA core courses only.

For more information, visit the NCAA Eligibility Center website at www.eligibilitycenter.org.

Young Adult

I remember visiting and writing my oldest brother in prison.

I remember realizing and accepting that I would not have a future in the NFL.

I remember my last college game and practice.

I remember feeling like I would never graduate with my Bachelor's Degree.

I remember thinking that guys in the street have more money than me.

I remember guys in the street driving better cars than mine.

I remember driving the Ford Tempo. It broke down in the Wendy's drive-thru. I held up the line. Everyone blew the horn at me and my car.

I remember my mom and dad arguing. My mom tried to hide the fact they were having problems because I was away at college.

I remember my mom and dad getting a divorce.

I remember my dad losing his business.

I remember my dad affair tearing apart our family.

I remember the shame and guilt my mom felt.

I remember losing our house to foreclosure.

I remember moving back home. Home no longer felt like home.

I remember being unhappy with my mom and dad.

I remember driving my 2006 Lincoln Zephyr off the lot.

I remember my 1st day of work at Wolverine Human

VIIII   Chapter 9

Growing up without Role Models

Generational Disconnect and Bridging the Gap

Remember the days of long ago; Think about the generations past. Ask your father, and he will inform you. Inquire of your elders, and they will tell you.
Deuteronomy 32:7

Life is not about being great every second. Sometimes I want to be silly, sometimes I want to be wrong, sometimes I want to have a neutral conversation with my elders.

"**R**espect your elders." I was taught that at a very young age. As a young adult I continue this practice. Generational Disconnect is loaded with ambiguity. There are various disconnects between various groups. Social media would be an example. Some prefer Facebook while others prefer Twitter or LinkedIn. Those in their 20's prefer the club over the church. Not all but the majority. The communication gap and generational disconnect I'm most alarmed by is the one between the young and the wise (old) men.

I enjoy talking with my elders. I truly feel they have something to offer, if they choose to share. Now-a-day, for whatever reason, men are reluctant to share their wisdom. Some men have abandoned "showing" and "teaching." Some have taken the stance "earn your stripes." I never quite understood why the wise would take their wisdom to the grave and refuse to share it. One's legacy is as much about what he has done as it is about what he has shared through communication.

It is believed that the older generation wants the younger generation commonly referred to as the Millennial generation (Generation Y) to go through the same thing they went through to get to where they are today. I don't believe all of my elders carry this belief but the reality is some do. I believe what our forefathers endured was intended to benefit today's generation and in many ways it has. Because of them, I was able to attend college, work for myself and create my own business among other things.

I would like the men before me to share their story, make us understand. Command that we listen. I would like the men before me to assume we care and want to know about the struggle, about their journey. If you are alive to tell it, why not let it be known. We live in the "information world" but yet we know very little or very little about what really matters. Men should present themselves at every street corner and liquor store to tell their story. They should visit the prisons and detention centers to enlighten that population as well. Change only happens when we orchestrate it. As a facilitator of change, you have to be willing to lend your time, treasure and talent. You have to be willing to share your story and continue to tell it even when it appears they are not listening. We have to be relentless in our pursuit of change. We have to be consistent. Today's generation expects inconsistency and limited follow through. We have to show them differently by being the change we intend to see.

I notice that men today are not present. Not all men, but most men. Many boys grow up without a father. Many boys struggle to become productive men. Many fathers fail to raise their son to be a young man. Many factors contribute to the father-son relationship or lack thereof. Our Black men, our fathers are disproportionately placed in prisons throughout the country. Many men, who now occupy a cell in State or Federal Confinement did not have or know their father. They have kids while living a life of crime and the cycle continues.

I've always understood the importance of a strong father or male figure in a child's life. We lack positive male influences in our communities and the only model kids have to look toward are the neighborhood D-Boys and gang members. When a kid removes his eyes off of them, the T.V. shows them a more successful version of their neighborhood idol perpetuating a cycle and a false truth.

My challenge to the men before me is to find one kid to wrap your arms around and take under your wing. Teach him everything you know. Show him how to live righteous but understand we are all fallible. Teach him to respect women and children by showing him how it's done. In my pursuit of challenging men, I often ask them have they passed their wisdom down onto the next coming, onto the future, onto tomorrow's leaders. I make sure they understand that no one wins if you take all of your knowledge to your grave and fail to pass on things that could lead to a better life for someone else. In talking with older people, I've notice they are reluctant to pass down their experiences, their wisdom. In talking with them, I could never figure out why.

Millennials or those born in the 80's and 90's may be to blame for our elder's reluctance. Many of us present with a cocky arrogance, we lack humility and overall knowledge of our history as people and strides made to give us life as we know it today. Some believe we walk around with a sense of entitlement. Others believe we are flat out lazy and lack ambition. Regardless of one's perception of my generation, I see teachable moments. I understand that regardless of one's perception, we are all created in God's image. The reality is, most men representing Generation X, which are those born in the 60's and 70's spent an ample amount of time in jail or prison. They are known in some circles as the "Absent Generation." Many of them did not exist. This was largely due to long stretches in correctional facilities. This unfortunate reality created a gap, a dissonance, a divide.

Most of us were raised by our grandparent's. Some lived with family members such as aunts and uncles. The true sense of family was lost. We no longer ate at the table for dinner or watched movies together. Instead we chose to hang with friends or play video games in our rooms. We lost the ability to communicate effectively. Our history and ancestry was perceived as old, or back then and no longer had relevance to our generation. Our elders turned bitter and cold. We turned defiant and oppositional. Respect was lost, there was no one to mediate or bridge the gap. The dissonance continued. We developed our own independence and sense of self and begin to display a willful disregard for our grandparent's, Malcolm, Martin and Marcus.

Today's youth are growing up fast in a world that is a lot different from our parents. We live in a world of instant gratification, immediacy. Some circles refer to us as the "Microwave Generation." Not only do we want things now, we want them right now. Many of us expect it. Many of us demand it. When things don't go our way, we snap, we get angry, we become disrespectful. These reactions to being told "No" or having to delay or wait, is why our elders feel we think we're entitled. Financial strain, a weak economy and a 10% nationwide unemployment rate only strengthens the divide.

Social network sites such as Facebook, Myspace and

Twitter are causing other kids to keep up and live outside of their means. A kid see's something his friend or someone his age has and wants it. Kids are not considering their families circumstances. They don't understand. They feel that, because you are mom or dad or grandma you are supposed to get me what I want. They feel your main purpose is to provide their every want and need and when you don't or cannot, you are a bad parent. Some run away, some turned to the streets. Others rob, steal and sometimes kill. They have not been taught to wait or to be patient. Since a kid, they have gotten whatever they desired. Granted things were cheaper before they became teens, but nevertheless the enabling began long ago. Working or earning what they want is considered work and work is considered hard.

Men have to be present, not only to your son or daughter, but to those around and in your community. Mentors are important. Teachers are important. Coaches are important. It is up to individuals in those roles to show them the way. Don't assume kids today won't listen. Of course, trust needs to be established. A strong rapport is important. Work to create that link and go from there. Today's youth desire to be lead. Many have no direction. What is sad is the ones they are choosing to follow are the only ones who have extended their hand. Today's youth must be challenged, coached and called. As men we have to challenge them, question their motives and dispute their beliefs, respectfully. We have to coach them. This includes showing them and not just telling them how to be men or how to avoid the penitentiary. The final thing we must do as men is to call them. Calling our youth or following up with them, making sure they are attending school and applying themselves, making sure they have someone to count on when things become difficult at home or in their personal life. I call this practice the Three (3) C's. I preach it everywhere I go. In addition to challenging men to be present, once present we must coach and call our youth. This will start the healing process. This will help bridge the gap.

Live Fast, Die Young

Y.O.L.O. also known as You Only Live Once is a popular phrase used by those living life on the edge. In the urban community, many of us know all-too-well about living on the edge but see you can't live wrong and receive God's blessing. God does not hear your prayer if you stay in rebellion. The concept of Y.O.L.O is not to smoke, drink and become a complete fool. It's to go out and do something with your life that truly matters. Wrong has become the new best practice. But see wrong is not the norm. It's just the accepted way of living. The people did whatever seemed right in their own eyes. - Judges 21:25

Be careful how you live. Short term conquest leads to long term defeat. There is truly no need to live fast. We must wait on God's appropriate time. Don't move until God tells you to move. The faith-walk is a marathon, not a sprint. Don't get weary in well-doing.

Slow down. Strive to earn God's trust. Show that you can be faithful over a few things first. He can't use you if He can't trust you. It's hard to build trust living fast. Living fast is often the result of living reckless. God has plans for you to prosper. He never intended for you to live fast and die young. Typically those who live fast to die young lacks hope and a person who lacks hope typically lacks vision.

Thank God for my momma and daddy

My mom and dad are my biggest role models. No matter where I go, people have nothing but good things to say about them. My mom, Glorie Sain is by far the sweetest person on earth. She is caring and loves to give. Family means a lot to her and for her family she will do whatever it takes to provide or support us. She was a secretary for Grand Rapids Public Schools for 10+ years. Kids and fellow staff members absolutely love her. I had over 100 friends by 6 years old because of her and these were kids that attended her school, not my elementary school. No matter if you were young or old, black or white, people, especially students gravitated towards her. Til' this day people talk about how nice my mom was. She is the type of person people will always remember.

I consider my mom a hard worker. She is an expert with the softer side of nurturance. She has always been loyal to her job and to her family. My mom would give her last to help someone else. She has a very giving heart. What I love most about her is her sense of humor and her resilience. I've seen her endure a lot. What most people don't know is she has a very silly side. Plenty of days as a kid growing up she would imitate my grandmother and other people. She can sound like anyone. I've always projected that in another life she would be a comedian or a movie actress doing voice-overs for animated films. As a family we have been through a lot but through it all she remained strong. Through it all she is still standing and making a difference in the lives of others. She attended every one of my Football and Basketball games since I was eight years old. I knew when she arrived to the game because she was always the loudest parent.

My dad, Chris Sain Sr. is special as well. He was a non-traditional father that instilled a lot of values and principles in me at an early age. He talked to me like an adult from the time I was born. I think that is how I became so mature at a very young age. Growing up, I never heard the goo-goo-ga-gah talk. The cutesy baby lingo did not exist in our household. My dad was all business every day, seven days a week; *Power-Suit* and *Power-Tie* described him best. He was very influential and charismatic at the same time. He was a dad that loved his boys dearly. My dad taught me life lessons that school, college or my corporate life never did. He prepared me for rainy days and taught me how to dance in the rain. I am named after my dad. Expectations for me were high, especially as a kid. I did things other kids did. I did age appropriate things but I could never get too far into kiddy land because of my dad and his prominence in the community. I had to carry his name, the weight associated with it, as well as make a name for myself along the way.

My dad, like other men made mistakes. We are all fallible, even dads. I learned a lot from the mistakes he's made. I learned what not to do. His good outweighed his bad but often people tend to focus on the mishaps. He had the best poker face on earth. I could never tell when things bothered him; well sometimes I could but not often. He dealt with a lot. He was constantly fighting an uphill battle. He was an entrepreneur that did not have a college degree. He clawed his way to the top and entered the back doors instead of the front. His struggles and obstacles taught me the importance education. He told me that I could avoid the obstacles he faced by going to college and getting my degree. High School was a prerequisite, college was mandatory. I told my dad to maintain his health because I would do great things in my lifetime and I wanted him to be able to witness my success. That was a promise I made to him when I was 18. I'm sure he is proud of the person I've become and the things I have accomplished. He is proud I am his son, his namesake.

Childhood Hero (Athlete)

Emmitt Smith – I thank God for NFL Hall of Fame running back, 3 time Super bowl Champion and All-Time NFL Leading Rusher. As a kid, he gave me someone positive to emulate on and off the field. I wore number 22 and scored countless touchdowns in hopes of making you proud. Although I have never met you, you forever remain my childhood sports hero. Thanks being a positive example for not only myself, but urban youth across the country on what it is to be a true professional.

X   Chapter 10

Dare to be Different

Be the Best Version of You

*Therefore, come out from among them and separate
yourselves from them, says the Lord. Don't touch their
filthy things, and I will welcome you.*
2Corinthians 6:17

Transition from fitting in to standing out!!!

Consecrate yourself!

Many people are afraid to emulate righteousness.
Not sure if you know it, but you are fearfully and
wonderfully made. I am blessed and because I am
blessed, I desire to be a blessing to others. There was a
point and time in my life when I did not know who I
was. See, my identity was wrapped up in what I did,
which was football, which became who I thought I was.
Before I formed a relationship with the Lord, I did not
know God created me in His image. I remember at one
point chasing a *look of success* or what I believed to be
socially accepted by the world. During that time, I did
not know God. I turned my back on God and therefore
God could not trust me. He could not trust my flesh. He

could not trust me with finances. He could not trust me with women...

When God can't *trust you*, He can't *use you*!

I learned this the hard way. Many people see the end result but very few consider the journey. I have learned to embrace the grind, while enjoying the climb. Can God trust you? For me, I was determined to get in right standing with the Lord. I had gone hard for the other side for so long and it got me nowhere. I decided it was time to try something different. It was at that moment that I consecrated my life and made up in my mind that I was going to go just as hard for the Kingdom. See, I did so much to embarrass the Kingdom I didn't think it was possible for God to use me or forgive me. But along the way, after reading my bible and getting to know Jesus, I found out that His mercies are renewed daily. His blessings are new every morning.

God has a plan for your life. He has plans to see you prosper. I followed my own plan for the longest before realizing that my plan was not leading me anywhere. It was not until I asked God to show me the way I began to see change. I asked God to give me the desires of my heart and He told me He would, if I allowed Him to order my steps. See, as a ball player, I thought it would be my athletic gifts and abilities that would take me places. I thought football was not only my ticket out of my environment but also my ticket to traveling and financial prosperity. Boy was I wrong. I had it all wrong. I must say sports, football in particular played a huge role in my life, but God had different plans for my life. God's plan for my life included much of the same except, a football was not involved nor was a career as a high profile athlete or the platform you get when you become a professional athlete. God was more concerned with me getting to know him. He promised to make my name great.

Once God knew He could trust me, He knew he could use me...

I will admit I am the guy who was most unlikely to graduate from college. I didn't even like school but because God loved me, He saved me from myself. He saved me from my own ignorance. I ask that you refrain from recognizing me, but to recognize God. I give Him all the praise. To God be the Glory.

Living a Vibrant Christian Faith

We are sinners saved by grace through faith, well at least I am. When I found out about God's forgiveness and how much he loved me, I was happy. I was relieved on the inside. A weight was lifted. I started going hard for the Kingdom to represent all He is. Seriously! I had done so much "wrong" I didn't think there was a place for someone like me. I thought to myself, "How could He use me? I sin daily." See, but once I began to chase after His heart, dive deeper into the word (Bible) and get some understanding, I learned, or should I say, I discovered that I was a representative of God. Thank

God for Forgiveness-Favor-and-Deliverance.

Suggestions to Achieve a Vibrant Christian Faith

- ☐ Seek a Spiritual Mentor or Coach
- ☐ Get some Accountability Partners
- ☐ Allow yourself to be challenged by others
- ☐ Attend worship beyond just Saturday & Sundays
- ☐ Seek Holiness not Happiness
- ☐ Be willing to walk alone
- ☐ Pray daily individually
- ☐ Form a prayer group
- ☐ Carve out space and time for God, don't rely on free time
- ☐ Show Compassion to God's People

Come out from among them

See, a long time ago I knew God had a plan for my life. But, because I was not listening, the plan was never fully revealed to me. It amazes me that He's brought me this far with little compliance. If you knew me in my madness, I would have been described as non-compliant or better yet, incorrigible. I began to imagine what was in store for me once I submitted, became fully committed and began to listen. God's grace is sufficient. His grace did allow me to have some small victories in my life. On some levels, I did experience small levels of success but never to the extent that I knew it could be. One day I cried out to the

Lord. I began to say "Speak Lord, ya boy (servant) is listening." I said, "Lord, I'm listening, speak to me." Looking back it's funny, but I figured out that, God will not answer, if you don't ask the question? The Bible says, Faith comes from hearing, and hearing comes from the word of God. In order to hear from God, you have to spend time with him. I have noticed, when I'm not in God's word on a regular basis, I go back to bad habits. *Bad habit's* often leads to storms in our life. 90% of the storms in our life are caused by us. All storms we face however should not be seen as bad. Your storm is a part of God's script. It's His way of testing your character and faith. I've found out that not only am I responsible for most, if not all the storms in my life but that it was also God's way of getting my attention. I've noticed that sometimes we give God the least amount of time making everything else more important. As Christians, sometimes we refuse to purge ourselves from our love affair with the world. At some point we must transition from fitting in, to standing out also known as coming out from among them. When I refused to listen, I was back at square one, this time asking "Lord, show me a sign that your favor is still on my life."

Be Who You Are Called To Be Without Compromise

My anointing is not in a title. It is in who I know. I am who I am and I happen to do a number of different things with the gifts God has given me. I am what God has made and I let that be known everywhere I go. God ain't done with me yet. As a matter-a-fact, He is just getting started. God told me, it is not my place to describe myself because that is what my gifts will do. "You will know the tree by the fruit that it bears", therefore you will know who I am and what I am about, by what I do with my life. It is true that "Your Actions will always follow your Beliefs." So find your purpose and live out your purpose. The door I walked through might not be for you and that's okay. Find your purpose. Remember when you do, not everyone is going to be happy for you. Walk it out anyway!!! Prepare yourself! There will be some people who won't embrace the "New You"....but so what. Remember, God gave you the vision, not them. Check this out, when you are operating in your Purpose, even your mistakes work toward your good. God helps those who help themselves. So don't just pray, take action. *Living in Faith* is not comfortable. But God knows that...but see favor is only obtained through obedience.

Know you circle. You cannot hangout with negative people and expect to have a positive life. When you are living a vibrant Christian life, not everyone will understand where you are going. So what! Love them anyway and remember to always be *compassionate* to

Gods people. You will one day realize, the people you want most in your life, are sometimes the people you are best without. Everybody won't understand your vision and that's okay. The Faith-Walk is a marathon. I use to complain about how people only saw the end result but never considered the journey. It was almost as if I resented the journey. But through seeking wise counsel, I received clarity. When I think about the Lord and the things I am thankful for, I now say "Lord, I want to thank you for the journey."

Things to remember when seeking to live righteous

- Your character will always outweigh your credentials.
- Nothing changes if nothing changes.
- The Son of Man did not come to be served, He came to serve. So, it is your duty to serve.
- Can you work when nobody celebrates you?
  Check your motives
- Be encouraged daily because your yesterday doesn't matter to Him. His mercies are renewed daily.
- Stop focusing on your limitations. With God, all things are possible.
- Your pain becomes your energy. Let your pain push you to greatness.
- I am who I am. I was who I was...and I'm ok with both of those people.

- Those who leave everything in God's Hand will eventually see God's hand in everything.
- Be careful how you live.
- You have outgrown other people's expectations of you.
- Can God get an Hour of your time? Don't rely on "free time" carve out space.
- Your anointing is not in your title. It's in who you know (God).
- Do that thing that's on your heart every day!! That's your ticket to peace & prosperity!
- Be thankful for what you have; you'll end up having more. If you concentrate on what you don't have, you will never, ever have enough.
- Be the Best Version of You. Everybody else is already taken.

Pursue your passion

Let another praise you, and not your own mouth; a stranger, and not your own lips

– Proverbs 27:2

Idolatry:

At some point, we have to figure out what we are passionate about and what our purpose in life is. For some, purpose and passion is discovered through life experiences and for others it is revealed to them. When pursuing your passion, make sure nothing separates you from the love of God. Make sure that your passion is connected to your purpose but that it is not something that supersedes your relationship with God. Why? Because anything that you love more than God, becomes your idol! For example, lust of the eyes has become your God. Your Pastor has become your God, your favorite singer or rapper. Weed has become your God. Pornography has become your God. For others, working out, training and lifting weights has become your God. Basketball, football, baseball, and your favorite player, has become your God. The video game for some, have become your God, your idol. We serve a jealous God, a God that desires to have all of your heart. Put nothing above God because when you do, it becomes your idol.

Idolatry is the universal human tendency to value something or someone in a way that hinders the love and trust we owe to God. It is an act of theft from God whereby we use some part of creation in a way that steals the honor that is due to God. Idolatry conflicts with our putting God alone first in our lives, in what we love and trust. In your spare time read Exodus 20:3-5; Deuteronomy 5:7-9; Romans 1:21-23 for a deeper look.

In idolatry we put something or someone, usually a gift from God, in a place of value that detracts from the first place owed to God alone, the gift Giver. That thing or person is an idol. The way out of idolatry is always to love and to trust the gift Giver without interference from any gift or anything other than God. We will then be able to love and to appreciate gifts appropriately, neither giving them too much power nor failing to be thankful for them. We will then be free and not in bondage to anything that cannot fulfill us.

Putting God first means loving and trusting God first, above all, and with everything we are and have (read Deuteronomy 6:5; Matthew 22:37; Mark 12:30; Luke 10:27). God has given us every good thing we have. Our focus should never be on the gifts themselves in a way that demotes the gift Giver. This would be idolatry. It is easy to see how idolatry occurs given our deadly propensity for selfishly willful control. In idolatry we fail to give proper thanks to the Giver of life and its goods. As thieves we steal God's rightful honor and diminish fellowship with both God and others. Our idolatry brings us under God's judgment, for our own good as seen in Romans 1:21-32. His judgment calls us from death to life and forces us to do His will, His way.

Giving up idolatry requires letting go of any and all possessive attitudes toward the gifts given to us. This allows us to receive the gifts not on our terms but on the terms of their ultimate Giver. This is the key to freedom in life under God, the ultimate gift Giver. God proves His love for us by sending us Jesus to befriend us, even to die for us in self-giving love. The provision of this unconditional, unearned love offers the kind of satisfying friendship that makes idols pointless and even repulsive. It frees us from idols in order to enable us to love as Jesus loves. In accepting Jesus as Lord, we discover the key to freedom. We find freedom to live in uncompromised love as we receive God's love freely.

Remember where you come from

Success will take you places you never imagined. Regardless of where it takes you, remember where you came from. Sometimes we have to look back to see how far we have come. Reflect on the journey and the challenges you had along the way. Everything you go through is for a reason. God designed it that way. He made it so you have something to talk about once you reach the top. There is joy in the climb. Remember to embrace the grind and enjoy the climb.

Sometimes we have to think about where we came from to remember where we are going. Our destination is often inspired by the things we have overcome. Along your journey there were traps and other things to cause you to abort your purpose. We lose friends along the way. We fall out with family along the way. It's called life. Everybody is not authorized to go where you are going. When God removes people from your life, let them go. They are gone for a reason. To get to where you are trying to get to, you need people around you that are willing to help you get there. It is important to remember those who helped you along the way. Nobody ever saw Glory without the help of someone else. Michael Jordan had Pippen. Kobe Bryant had Shaq. Always pay homage to those who helped you on your journey. It's the ultimate way to show your appreciation.

XI   Chapter 11
<u>Athletes and Depression</u>

Life after Sports

> *[17] For our present troubles are small and won't last
> very long. Yet they produce for us a glory that vastly
> outweighs them and will last forever! [18] So we don't
> look at the troubles we can see now; rather, we fix our
> gaze on things that cannot be seen. For the things we
> see now will soon be gone, but the things we cannot see
> will last forever. - 2 Corinthians 4:17-18*

There is more to life than sports...but not much

Foreclosed Identity is what we, most athletes suffer
from. A foreclosed identity is more commonly defined
as, what you do is who you are. Until further educated,
many athletes believe this to be true about them-selves.
I did. Who we are is tied to what we do. Ask most
athletes who they are? And most answers will be; "I'm
a football, or basketball or baseball player - or - I'm a
college athlete or a professional athlete." Although that
answer might be true on a surface level for many
athletes, especially given the context the question was
asked in, it is the farthest thing from the truth. Football,
basketball, baseball, etc. is what you do, not who you
are. I later learned it's what I did, not who I was. A lack
of knowledge about who I was aided my slip into
depression.

A false sense of self and of who I really was, led to the next detriment of myself and most athletes; Under-socialized. Many of us, athletes especially, are under-socialized. Like thousands of others athletes, I became obsessed with being the best at my given sport, this caused me to neglect the other aspects of life and the things that makes a person a well-rounded individual. This is also the number one reason it hurts so bad when I fail short, didn't actually make it or fulfill my athletic goals. Under-socialized in a number of life areas, to reach my athletic goals, I had to sacrifice other parts of my life. Why? Because of what sports demanded of me to be great at what I did. Because of the possibilities associated with being the best at what I did, along with the financial benefits and the ability to achieve the American Dream.

Sports, considered to be "just a game" or "entertainment" to others, became all-consuming. As a result, I did not mature and hit developmental milestones at the same rate of others. Feeling inadequate, like something was missing, sports conditioned me to wear a facade. Why? Because on the other side of blood-sweat-and-tears, I was going to be a professional athlete! See, a few missed developmental milestones get overlooked when you are a high profile athlete. Celebrity, power and new found wealth, qualifies you for a free pass (i.e. NFL Card). Most athletes don't have a date with the Super Bowl. Instead, most athletes have a date with depression. For me she was disguised as sleep, lack of motivation and isolation.

A non-stop replay of how I was affected by injuries, lack of playing time, not reaching my personal athletic goals played time and time again in my head. For me, my shoulder injury was the one injury that derailed my career the most. Too much time in the training room is never a good thing from an athlete's perspective. Why? A player's best ability is availability.

Most people struggle with change and transition. Take displaced workers for example. Displaced workers are workers who have been on the job 10, 15, 20, 25 plus years only to see the company dissolve and/or resurface overseas. These workers often struggle with learning new skills, finding a job with equal or greater pay and adjusting to the uncertainties of life that was once foreign to them because of the sense of security their job provided. These workers share a similar experience to what athletes face at the conclusion of their career. Whether that career is short-lived, never got started or was Hall of Fame worthy, when it's over it's over. It is the scariest time of most athletes' life. Like displaced workers, athletes very rarely successfully transition.

ESPN does not feature athletes who don't make it. We very seldom hear about those guys. You never hear about the reality of college and professional athlete's life after sports, how difficult the transition really is and the cognitions one has during the journey. By the time our stories are told it's too late. A self-inflicted gunshot wound is usually the headline or bankruptcy, foreclosures or divorce. No one has ever really seemed to shed light on the actual journey and no one tells the story of those who are able to make the transition. Much like workers who watch their jobs go overseas, you never hear about the worker and the struggle endured during the transition. Most people see the end result, but very few consider the journey.

Gone Forever

My college career was hardly anything to write home about. The way my career went helped me fully know that without a doubt, I simply loved the game. How could I not after the type of career I had? I reached a point where I simply played for the love of the game. It definitely was not because of winning or lots of playing time. No story book ending over this way. The days, weeks and months after my final game, the minute I realized that it was over, I am talking about when the reality officially set in, I was consumed with thoughts of what's next? Overwhelmed by the "What ifs?" and coulda-woulda-shouldas. Most days are spent moping around, trying to rearrange your life in a way that it doesn't come remotely close to reflecting the life of an athlete. It takes months sometimes years to bury what you use to be. For me it felt like a lifetime. Moving on from your old life, your life as an athlete is never ending it seems. The brotherhood, the fun times in the locker room serves as small reminders that make it increasingly hard to move on. It represents everything good about the game, when the game was pure and less about politics, so, to forget about that, you bury them by finding something else to be passionate about, hoping that you'll one day forget about what use to be. To be honest, I have felt many emotions since the end of my football career: hope and anger, disappointment, joy and despair. But, none stronger than the feelings of shame and embarrassment! It's been tough.

I tried to play it off as best as I could by putting on *50 Shades of Happiness*. The front, the façade, it was getting harder to keep up. I was miserable. Everything lost meaning. Nothing really mattered. In my presence, it was not hard to tell I wasn't happy. Daily I would think and say to myself, "I would give up everything to go back and play the game of football." With each passing day, month and year, it seems as if for whatever reason you just don't get over it. The feeling never goes away. You simply learn to live with it. Nostalgia best described the feeling.

Although my playing days are long over, the competitiveness stills lives within me. It is still there. I struggle between healthy and unhealthy competition. The fire remains, which is why I am constantly searching for positive outlets, at the gym, working out, writing or on other areas I am gifted in. I left it all on the field. Everything I had. The sad thing is the urge, the thought; the love of the game won't leave me. See, sports for me, had become my refuge, you know, the place where I was in my true element. I found peace with football and basketball.

As everything stops, I'm left sitting on the edge of my bed wondering where to turn. Every day I look in the mirror I am trying to figure out how I can find peace in the next chapter of my life. How can I enjoy the next half of my life without the thought of what should've been, flooding my mind? What else am I passionate about? How can I find passion and purpose in other areas of my life, in things that don't involve sports? What about peace? How do I find peace away from the game?

Due to my foreclosed identity I had come to find out that, I never knew peace. At the time, I was under-socialized. I was obsessed with sports but I didn't really know God. He was not in any of what I was doing or what I was trying to pursue. Girls occupied whatever time I had left and could have made for the Lord. The way my career went, I didn't even reach low level fame or notoriety. Not only did I not have peace I was plagued with bitterness and resentment. Who I was, was wrapped up into what I did. Outside of sports, I had no true identity. The game itself brought me a sense of purpose and gave me an identity, so I thought. I later realized I had neither. I learned further down the road that purpose and identity is not accessible through sports. What I was after was only accessible through the Son of the Holy Spirit.

Why Me

Pitiful, sad, abandoned and lonely; at the time those words described me best. I was hopeless. I was left with all the feelings, feelings I wouldn't wish on anybody. Looking back, from the start it was bad. I looked so forlorn, so empty like the life had been sucked out of me. Why me? I wasn't heavily recruited, scholarship offers passed me by. Why me? I arrived on campus taking a full load (12 credit's/Full-Time Student), dropped a class and unbeknownst to me the minute you drop under 12 credit's you are ruled Academically Ineligible. Why me? I was constantly slowed by a shoulder injury that did not allow me to play to my potential. In the culture of college football, a player's best ability is availability. Why me? Why me I asked. I asked over and over in search of answer that would make all the pain go away. Why do some people catch a break and others don't? How come I never caught a break? Why do the people who put in the least amount of work get the best opportunities? Why do I work twice as hard as everyone else and receive half the credit and praise? Why am I going through this? Why?

Athletes who identities are directly tied to what they do (sports) are unaware of their true self outside of the game. These types of people have a strong *Athletic Identity*. They see themselves only as "football" or "baseball or "basketball players." They see themselves only as athletes unless somewhere along the way they've developed other areas of interest, they have good friendships or aspirations outside of sports, it can be quite painful, adjusting to life after sports as it was for me and plenty others.

As for star athletes when the final whistle of their career blows, it is common that many will be leaving their sport without anything to bolster their next career, nothing of interest to them, nothing that they were anticipating pursuing while still actively playing the game. Many athletes are then stuck, asking the same question. Where do I go from here?

Some retiring athletes as well as the ones who simply didn't make it, can suffer depression. I was one who didn't make it in a sense, according to my standards. According to the goals I set for myself as an athlete. When the game is your love, your passion, no matter what level you reached, it is a struggle for us all when it's over. We become depressed. Depressed is a word commonly associated with women, so for strong, mighty men, it is easy to dismiss the feelings and replace it with words like; *frustrated* or *lack of motivation.*

Going back to a normal life may run more smoothly for athletes who go into coaching, return to school or those with a day job. It provides a sense of belonging. It provides structure and something to do temporarily for the time being. For those who have never worked a traditional job, the task might be more challenging. The bottom line is that in general many athletes tend to neglect the next chapter of their life; "Life after Sports." Many athletes just simply fail to plan their next career move. The gift and the curse for most athletes is that they only focus on their athletic goals, which is why some become great and don't think about what comes after. By the time some athletes start thinking about it, it's too late.

When the game is over, often times there is nowhere to turn for help. Many athletes try to find their own way. Academics is an option but athletes feel out of touch and too far removed in a classroom setting. However, well-versed and well-educated athletes can often end up having a vibrant life as a working professional. But sometimes, no matter what their background, athletes fail to adapt to their new life as retired athletes or athletes that don't make it. Some athletes search their whole life trying to find the next best thing, something to replace the game, but provide a similar rush. Very few find it and end up going down several dead end roads. There is nothing that I have found that compares to competing in sports and doing what you love. "But family, friends and the fans at home watching don't see all that goes into the game, the pain and the injuries, the sacrifice. More than anything else, sports provide a real outlet for your competitive juices. With nothing to replace the feeling with, the stark reality is that most athletes go into depression.

Letter

November 28th, 2006

Dear Football,

"*I just played my last college football game. We are done! It's over! Dream unfulfilled!!!*"

Along with basketball you were my first true love. I gave up everything to be with you. I sacrificed fun for hard work. I replaced partying with pain because for me, pain was nothing more than weakness leaving the body. While others were taking shortcuts, trying to cheat the grind, I worked while everybody else was asleep. I've tried hard to get over you but the pain is real. The hurt is real. I even stopped going to the barbershop because of you. What I'm going through, Arm-Chair Quarterbacks, Sweat Suit All-Americans and Barbershop ESPN Analyst wouldn't understand. I'm mad and confused. Most nights I can't sleep. It's hard to watch games because I see it differently than the average person. I'm not a fan. I'm not a sports critic. Playing ball is what I do. It's who I am.

I still can't figure out why it never worked out. Wrestling with this thought keeps me up at night. Since a kid, somewhere around 8 years old I had the ability to envision all of my touchdowns and big plays I would make the nights before and during the game. When my number was called I knew specific times I would score a touchdown. At running back, five to six yards deep looking out at the defense, I actually saw the big play before it happened. I arrived at Michigan State University (MSU) as a kid who was not highly recruited coming out of high school. I didn't care. Playing against some of your favorite players, I did my thing. I learned that hard work beats talent when talent doesn't work hard. As a Defensive Back I would pick Drew Stanton off almost every day and every other quarterback, wherever I played in college. The funny thing was, just like when I was a kid, I envisioned it. I knew the night before that at our next practice during team, 1-on-1 or 7-on-7 I would get a pick. I left MSU and it was more of the same at Grand Rapids Community College (GRCC) and Saginaw Valley State University (SVSU). But in the end it just didn't work out.

Why? It's a question I often ask myself. Left searching for answers I get mad and frustrated all over again. Why? Because I gave you (the game of football) more than what you gave me in return. I have never been to the Circle City Classic. Why? Because it was during the season! I didn't take trips and do the regular stuff that regular kids experienced. Why? Because I was certain that football would pay off. You were my ticket to traveling the world. The blood-sweat-and-tears I invested didn't produce a good return at all. All of this work for nothing. Now, I sit here contemplating the next chapter of my life, lost with no direction and constantly asking "what's next for me?" and "where do I go from here"? So many people were depending on me. I can't afford not to make it. It was over. I'm so mad at the outcome of my career I can't even think about the good times along the way with you. I put my cleats on, helmet and shoulder pads on, for the last time and I will never forget taking my cleats off, my helmet off and my shoulder pads off for the last time. I have only cried once in my life but this is tough. I felt emotions I didn't even know I had. I'm now forced to try and find a regular job. It's tough because for 16 years football was my job. We hooked up when I was eight (8). This means I have to leave you for Education. She was never that appealing to me. This makes finishing up my bachelor's degree that much more important. Life without you will be tough but I have to move on now. I know there are other things out there that I'm good at. Just not sure I'll like it as much as you but although things didn't work out between us, every day since my career ended I check on you. Remember, nobody loved you more than me. Thanks to nfl.com and College Gameday, from afar, I can stay closely connected to the game.

Love,

Yours Truly

Chris Sain

XII   Chapter 12

<u>Vision creates Victory</u>

Beating the Odds

Never stop praying.

1Thessalonians 5:17

**"People don't care how much you know...until they
know how much you Care"** –

John C. Maxwell

Breaking the cycle of poverty, lack of education,
violence, and hopelessness: I'm no one special! I'm far
from perfect. I just know what I know. All of my life I
feared being called or considered a dumb athlete. I
feared it so much so, that it became my biggest
motivator. They say perception equals one's reality; I
tried hard to ensure no one perceived me as dumb. I'm
not sure why this notion held so much weight, but it did
and because it did, it has made me who I am. I walked
through life, or most of it believing a football player
was who I was. It was not until I realized football is
what I do, not who I am that my transformation began.

Yes, I am highly competitive and yes I compete and strive to be the best. I am in competition with no one. I have no desire to play the game of being better than anyone. I am simply trying to be better than the person I was yesterday. In the workplace I am dangerously ambitious and ooze with confidence yet I will never hoist the Super Bowl Trophy. My wins come in a different form. Sometimes my wins don't reveal itself until two or three years down the road. I've learned all about delayed gratification. I know what it is to plant seeds and wait. Working as a case manager, it is what I have come to expect.

I brought a swagger to college classrooms. That swagger followed me into the workplace. Well trained athletes perfect their craft. I am a professional now. Only 24, I have perfected my craft. Although there is still room for improvement and professional growth my drive, charisma and expectations coupled with book smart's suit's me well. The one constant in the professional world is that most people are extremely book smart. I assume professionals took really good notes in graduate school. It seems some have even memorized entire textbooks, all of them. I enjoy the intellectual conversations of colleagues. I laugh when conversations sound like a dissertation. Everyone likes to show off their new found wisdom, vocabulary and professional jargon.

Street smarts, book smarts and common sense sets me apart. In the professional arena, 9 out of 10 people are highly educated, well; at least they act like they are. I notice most are extremely book smart. But, I also notice that most find it difficult to hold meaningful conversations especially when the conversation does not revolve around their area of expertise. I notice many lack basic social skills. It's funny to think a person with a Ph.D. or Master's Degree lack these basics skills but it is true. Education only matters when you actually use it. It doesn't automatically make you smarter than someone. Some say knowledge is power. Knowledge is not power. However, applied knowledge is power. If a person reads and educates himself to be knowledgeable in certain areas, one could actually be more knowledgeable than someone with a degree. The most important thing about an education is commitment to self. To earn a degree requires sacrifice, time management, determination, perseverance and motivation. These are all traits that make you appealing to companies and organizations whether big or small. These traits are also transferrable and can make you a great entrepreneur as well.

My biggest fear had now become my biggest motivator. I was performing well in college and was considered a natural in my profession. I noticed no one perceived me as dumb. As a matter-a-fact, in 24 years, no one has ever said I was dumb. It dawned on me one day that I walked around most of my life fearful of being considered a dumb athlete and that was nowhere on anyone's radar. How could it be? In High School I maintained a 3.3 cumulative G.P.A. In college I was an Academic All-American. I consistently maintained a 3.6 or better. Grad School was more of the same. My G.P.A jumped to a 3.8. How could someone call me dumb? If the proof is in the pudding, the pudding indicates I was far from dumb.

Wayne State University (WSU) is where I attended graduate school. Wayne St. is located in Detroit, Michigan. I was the youngest person in my graduate program. Being the youngest was nothing new. I was also 1 of 3 males in the program. The program consisted of me, a white guy and Vincent, an older black guy who wanted to move up at his current place of employment. The rest of the program consisted of women, some older women and some younger or what many call non-traditional students. Nontraditional students are described as those who have returned to school to gain or acquire new skills, those who have been with their company several years and want to move up. I went to school to be a clinical therapist. I specialized in cognitive behavioral therapy (CBT). Substance use, Youth Services and Couples Therapy were other areas of study. Most of my classmates were twice my senior and had been in their respected profession for numerous years. They were experienced. They were experts at the workplace returning to school years later to advance, to experience upward mobility on the job.

Having children and providing shelter, clothing and food caused some to postpone their education. Many had to or chose to wait until their children were of age to return to school. Many nontraditional students experienced unemployment and lacked job opportunities while others suffered through a painful divorce or got married. Some experienced death of a loved one. Whatever the factors were altered the course of their lives. Years of being full time parents and professionals, they now return to school looking to better themselves, their situation and their families. Along the way, students who returned to school as seasoned adults were labeled non-traditional.

Considered young by most standards and by far one of the youngest in the program, I was concerned when I saw no one in the program that looked like me. I remember walking through campus saying to myself "So…am I the only one that wants to make a difference in the lives of others?" I remember vowing to influence others to go to school. I was saddened to know that I was the only *young-black-male* in the entire program at the time. Although saddened, I used the revelation as motivation. "I will be the only one under twenty-five graduating with a master's" I said to myself. "I will change the face of therapy" was my other internal motivator. Being young gave me an excuse to learn from my elders. During grad school I was like a sponge. I tried to soak up as much information about the real world as possible, knowing my time was coming soon. The more I sought to understand the more I realized how much I knew. The more I soaked up, the more I felt validated. The more I listened the more my confidence grew. At semester's end, that all had changed. By finals week they were seeking advice and guidance from me. Moments like that let me know that I would be okay. Moments like that offered me the confidence I needed to change the face of therapy and implement innovative approaches to cognitive therapy.

Sometimes I feel a Master's Degree affords me the opportunity to sit in endless meetings. But the one thing I have noticed, more than anything else is the respect and command I have during meetings. As it is often said in the workplace; "Chris, you are the expert, your professional judgment is most valued. Your professional judgment and your professional intuition is relied upon." I get up from meetings to take a moment to walk to the restroom. I look in the mirror and say wow. Wow. I still have to pinch myself to make sure it is me they are referring to as the expert. Remember, I feared being called a dumb athlete. It motivated me to do my best. Many now consider me an expert and my insight is relied upon to make life changing decisions for individuals and families. From dumb athlete to expert is now how I am perceived. Most would applaud the journey, me on the other hand refuse to consider myself an expert. I also know I'm not dumb. My biggest fear motivated me to be better than I could ever imagine. My biggest fear caused me to earn a bachelor's and master's degree. My biggest fear became my biggest motivator. Now I say "everything I'm not, made me everything I am."

Don't let your humble beginnings be an excuse to why you don't achieve.

Hopelessness best describes the inner-city of most urban communities. The key to making it out is to avoid letting the devil steal your vision. Vision keeps you focus. Vision gives you something to shoot for. Never become comfortable with low living. Let nothing about broken communities, impoverished neighborhoods, drugs, crime and failure satisfy you. Stay humble and hungry. Remain humble and hungry.

Even when my ego was low, I achieved the unachievable. Never let them see you sweat, is what I told myself. Make everything look easy, even if it's not. I was built to handle and overcome adversity. Let downs and disappointments are a part of our everyday life. I wanted my humble beginning to be the backdrop to my story. My humble beginnings were always meant to serve as a soundtrack to my testimony. Never was it meant to serve as an excuse.

Expect no one to feel sorry for you and your hardships. Your experiences mean very little to the next man. I found that out the hard way. I learned along the way that my journey was mine and mine alone. It was up to me whether or not I saw victory. In order to see victory I first had to define what victory was for me. Initially, it was making it to my 18th birthday. Once I accomplished that, victory became less about me and more about making others proud. I have learned the best way to say thank you to those who have helped you along the way, is by what you choose to do with your life. My neighborhood featured enough examples of failure and underperformers. I decided early on that I wanted to be different. I wanted to be a positive influence for others to look up to.

If no one believes in you, believe in yourself. In an environment where everyone has had their appointment with failure, sometimes it's hard to believe. Sometimes it is hard for even your closest family members to believe in you because many of them stopped believing in themselves long ago. As a whole, in many ways we have lost hope. Hope has been stripped from us and many are left simply not knowing what to do. We stop living and settle for simply existing. We become hopeless because the challenges become too much to bear. Just because hope does not exist around you, does not give you an excuse to give up hope. Regardless of your circumstance or the hand you were dealt, you must believe. You must keep hope alive. If no one believes in you, believe in yourself.

When nobody else believed in me, I believed in me. I thank God for those who prayed for me. I thank God every day for working on my behalf behind the scenes. There are days that I feel like giving up. Some days it's a struggle. Every day there is an attack on my purpose. The devil is upset that I've made it this far. I really made the devil mad when I side stepped the traps he placed in my neighborhood. Every day the devil is out to get me. The adversary is still trying to figure out how I escaped. I won't look back. I can't. I'm too excited about where God is taking me. For me, not being called a dumb-athlete was the motivation. The fear associated with that compelled me to accomplish the unthinkable. My biggest fear became my biggest motivator. If you are reading this, figure out your deepest fear and let it motivate you to be great. Let it inspire you to do all the things the world said you couldn't do. Fear of the Lord is the beginning of wisdom. Let your deepest fear, your insecurities and your imperfections motivate you. That's what I did.

Epilogue

My book is about the first twenty-four years of my life mainly because statistics suggested that urban African American males would be dead or in jail by twenty-five. I wanted to share my journey with you, to let you know that it is not mandatory we go to jail. Not only is jail not a requirement or prerequisite of an African American male, there is actually much more to life than what you might know. I would be remiss if I did not share what my life has been like since then. Little did I know, God was just getting started with me!

After graduating from Wayne State University in May of 2008 with my MSW in Clinical Social Work, I jumped off the stage and days later tore my Achilles. With my NFL dreams and the salary that accompanies a professional athlete being a thing of the past at this point, I had to settle for a traditional job. Young with no insurance, I never knew crutches cost so much. I landed my first job, post master's degree, at Madison Center located in South Bend, Indiana. To make a long story short, I made more money in undergrad with no degree than I did here. How could this be? I have a master's degree. The only thing I could hang my hat on was my job title. I was a Clinical Therapist. It sounded good when telling it to friends and family, so good they wouldn't believe how much the salary was. At least Notre Dame was up the street.

Now 2009 and after about 6 months on the job, my Achilles was improving when another job opportunity presented itself. Two cities separated only by railroad tracks, I made my way over to Berrien Center, Michigan. The Berrien County Juvenile Center (BCJC) was looking for a Case Manager. The title initially threw me off but the $35,552 salary they were offering was much better than what I was currently making. I interviewed with about five people in a conference room; Teonna Wilber, Richard Dama, Terry Martinek, Kurt Struss and George Eddy. We talked briefly about the job but they were MSU fans (Mr. Dama in particular), I attended MSU, it was March Madness, MSU was playing, we started talking sports and the rest was history. I was hired on the spot. Well, they officially said that I would hear from them in two weeks, but by the time I made it to my car in the parking lot, the executive secretary had ran out to offer me the job.

Working at the BCJC with the city of Benton Harbor most at-risk teens really touched me in a way that inspired me to be more and to actually do more. The youth at the Juvenile Detention Center is really the target audience and who this book is intended for. Although universal in context and applies to people from all walks of life, I specifically had the BCJC youth and all at-risk youth around the country being warehoused in detention centers in mind. My role and involvement in their life was so vital. They depended on me. I could not afford to let them down. Those youth would soak up everything I told them, they would hang onto every word I said. That level of influence made it imperative for me to be the example that all urban at-risk youth could look to. I gave them hope. Through me, they could see themselves. I could tell they knew it was possible to achieve. I never missed a day of work. For many of the BCJC residents, it was the first time in their life they consistently saw a black man. I took that very seriously.

Connecting sports to all I do, I met a young lady named Jennifer Mockler-Grotegut at the BCJC who was a probation officer and a former athlete at Iowa State University where she ran track. I told her one day after court for a kid we were both representing, that if I ever left the BCJC my next job would be for the Detroit Lions working in Player Development. I told her I had already started investigating what I would need to do to land the job. Galen Duncan, Director of Player Development for the Detroit Lions and Detroit Pistons emailed me and told me to get as much experience as possible working with high school and college athletes. His advice was very helpful. Jennifer said well "my husband works with student athletes at the University of Notre Dame, I'll let him know what you're trying to do and I'll tell him to give you a call."

Chad Grotegut, Academic Counselor in Academic Services for Student Athletes Department gave me call. He immediately asked if I would be interested in meeting. Excited about the opportunity I said yes. We met at and he was accompanied by Adam Sargent. It was my first time interviewing for a job at a restaurant. I was excited. The three of us talked, we had a good time. After about two hours, they had heard all they needed to hear. They believed that my presence alone would increase the traffic and the amount of student-athletes that matriculated through the office. What they believed to be true, I knew was true. They hired me on the spot then immediately rushed back over to the Human Resources Department (HR) to acquire paperwork so that I could start ASAP. My title was Athlete Mentor. I was blessed to work with high profile student-athletes. These were not your typical student-athletes, these guys were borderline geniuses. To date, the University of Notre Dame staff is one of the best I've worked with. They also dispelled all assumptions I had about Notre Dame. They were all truly great people. Great as everyone were, it was apparent to me after a year at the college, that with or without me, these student-athletes were well to do. Knowing that many of the student-athletes came from supportive and affluent families, I made the decision in 2011 to return home to Grand Rapids, Michigan and serve a community that needed me more than my Notre Dame Students did. This meant I was also leaving the BCJC and all the kids I served there as well as their community. It was hard but it was time.

The next thing for me happened to be YouthBuild which is a program funded by the Department of Labor (DOL) targeting individuals 18-25 transitioning out of foster care, high school dropouts and at-risk youth looking for a life change. I was interviewed for the position and shortly named the Director. In about 6 months I had made great strides. For me, my sights were always set on Grand Rapids Community College (GRCC). If I did not make it professionally playing sports, it was always my goal to work at GRCC. I've always viewed GRCC as the hub for our community and if education is the key, I wanted to be there to assist community members turned students when they all arrived. But, for some reason I could never get a interview. For some reason, I could not figure out how to navigate their structure and infiltrate their hiring process. How could this be? I can work for any college in the country but I can't seem to generate any interest from the one institution I desired to work for most. Strange I thought. Even frustrating at times! I called my mom. She was part of the school system for 15+ years. I figured she'd know some folks. My mom knew Dave Selmon, a longtime friend, colleague and current Director at GRCC. She gave him a call and the rest was history. Thank God for my mom. She always comes through.

In the midst of all that was happening around me at the time, everything changed for me on October 10th, 2012. That was the day I married Corinthia, my wife, the love of my life, my rock and my crown. After a yearlong engagement, it was time. As a man you just know. We decided to make it official and something about it just felt right. For me, marriage is a big deal.

My past life tells a story of a true ladies man and marriage was not part of the script. In fact, I am the most unlikely guy of all to get married, but I must admit, it has been the best thing that has ever happened in my life. God has smiled on me and in marriage has afforded me opportunities that I could only dream of when I was living outside of His will. I have escaped the traps of the inner-city and have aligned myself to hear from God so that He could reveal the plans He has for my life. With so many young people running from marriage and choosing to shack up, what better example exist than my wife and I to show young people from all walks of life that marriage is the way to go.

For years I have offered my time, talent and treasure to others, surrounding cities and specifically to my community. Purpose eradicates need is what Grand Rapids own Rich DeVos once said. Unfortunately many urban communities lack purpose and hope. There is a need everywhere. I saw the need for someone like myself, young, urban, educated and accomplished, not only in Grand Rapids but also in Detroit, Saginaw, Benton Harbor, MI., Chicago IL, South Bend, IN and all over. I took my my story on the road. Working with youth and athletes and being respected in so many other communities I saw an opportunity. I began to speak all over the Midwest. By creating a buzz, I created a small demand. I believe everyone has a story. I worked hard to create a platform to share mine.

I speak at college campuses and universities, high

schools, urban high schools and to sports teams of all levels as well as prisons and other forms of correctional facilities. I speak to students, teachers, urban youth, suburban youth, educators and low hanging fruit on a regular basis. The irony in all of this is, I've done all of this without a book. That is nobody but God. At first I was hesitant when the phone calls and emails started coming in. Honestly, at first I contemplated turning down the invites. For me, all of the speaking was supposed to take place once my book was published. God was moving in a mighty way at the time. When the Lord is ordering your steps, you have no choice but to move when He says so. And that's what I did. I went from being an unpaid speaker, someone who started off speaking for free just because I knew somebody needed to hear from me, to now garnering $5,000 to $7,500. Many will say that my speaking fee is unheard of for an unpublished author when in reality what is unheard of is an African American male who eluded death and used book smarts, street smarts and common sense to graduate near the top of his class earning both bachelor's and master's degree by the age of twenty-four when most other African American males are dead or in jail by twenty-five. I have been described as uncommon or as an anomaly. My message resonates with audiences of all types. I am intentional about reaching urban youth at urban schools because I know how important it is for them to see some who looks like them, talks like them and truly understands their struggle. As an educator, I devote time to equipping educators with how to handle today's student, the hard to reach students with a diverse background.

I use sports and education as my vehicle to affect change. When speaking, sports analogies are injected into my message to deliberately depict how closely related life and sports are. No disrespect to any of my teachers, I had a few great ones along the way but sports were always my best teacher. Talking sports also keeps me loose and helps me relax. I am not a natural talker. I still get butterflies before speaking regardless the size of the audience. Schools across the country are cutting sports and forcing kids to pay to play. Many school officials are faced with trying to meet Annual Yearly Progress Goals as well as other benchmarks set by the state and sports has taken a back seat, obsolete even in some schools around the country. I use sports, in particularly football because it is the ultimate team sport. It teaches life skills vital to success and necessary for the real world.

Stay true to your brand. You are your brand. Stay true to who you are. Grand C.I.T.Y. is my brand, it's my passion. Helping people is what I do. Talking with others and getting to know people is what life is about. After all, life is about resources. Relationships equal Resources. Remember, it's not always about what you know sometimes it's about who you know. It is important to perceive yourself as a mentor or a role model. We are all role models or mentors to someone. Speaking to hundreds of people in a high school gym is no more important than quietly speaking to one. As long as my heart is in the right place when I speak, God will honor my efforts, which allows me to accomplish what was intended regardless if I am compensated fairly from a monetary standpoint.

When in meetings, or during intellectual conversations, it is often apparent that people associate money with power. Money, Power, Respect, are three words often associated with each other. It is my belief that it is more important to have influence than it is to have power which then makes *Respect* the ultimate currency. I expect Grand C.I.T.Y. to influence the life of young people but if that's all we do, and we fail to move people toward action and purpose, I'll have to re-evaluate the mission and the vision of the organization. Our faith based community driven nonprofit organization is designed to not only influence today's youth but positively impact the entire city of Grand Rapids and ultimately urban youth everywhere. Restoring the sense of community, developing civic leaders and responsible adults is the ultimate goal.

Understanding that life is not a race but more like a marathon helped me chart out my path to success and wealth. The 10 most important things I suggest for others while running the marathon is: 1. Trust in God. 2. Set realistic and attainable goals. 3. Think Big. 4. Visualize Success. 5. Believe in yourself. 6. Stay Focused. 7. Network. 8. Be a Leader. 9. Take Calculated Risk. 10. Have a desire to learn. The list is not pretty but unless you win the lottery or are in the real estate business when the market is good, I suggest following the 10 steps I have mentioned. Success comes in many forms. Everyday people can follow the blueprint and incorporate the steps mentioned while removing actor, movie star and professional athlete as your only way to achieve financial prosperity. We all begin each day with 24hrs. How you use your time is the only difference. I try to make every minute of every day count. I will continue to try to be extremely efficient with how I use my time.

Acknowledgements

The best way to say thank you, to those who have helped you along the way, is by what you do with your life

To God be the glory. His blessings are renewed daily. I just thank Him for dealing with me in private on my journey, allowing me the chance to grow without exposing me publicly. I still have a long way to go but I just want to say thank you. God is the creator of all things, therefore trust in the Lord with all your heart and lean not on your own understanding. Seek His will in all you do, and He will take care of all your arrangements.

The life experiences and urban perspective of this book have been divinely guided therefore I am forever grateful for my experiences and to those who have helped shape my views and perspective on life. I would first like to again, thank my Lord and Savior Jesus Christ for continuing to have uncommon favor over my life. I would like to thank Chris and Glorie Sain, my wonderful parents who raised me and helped me become the man I am today.

Special thanks goes out to my wife, Corinthia Sain. I want to personally thank you for being my rock and always supporting me. I want to thank my son, Anthony Collins for being a great kid and a hard worker. To Carlton Brewster and Eric Malloy: my best friends of over twenty years, A.J and Terna. Nande. Childhood Friends: Johnny "Hookem" Burress (my little brother), Shar, Randy, Ty, Cam Wilson, Dell Willis, Jerrell "Scoob" Calvert. Much love goes out to the "Magic-Bulls" and "The Regulators." My teammates at MSU, SVSU and GRCC as well as my high school and Rocket League Football teammates and coaches, everybody I played ball with at King Park, Mulick Park, Creston 78er's, AAU, Gus Macker's and Night Court at Paul I. Phillips.

Special thanks goes out to my brother, Jay (welcome home) proud of you and my baby brother Preston (proud of you too), my family, everybody in Muskegon. RIP to my Uncle Lee, Uncle Vern, Dahnontae McKinley, Derrick Pimpleton, Eddie Vander, Mr. Jordan and my grandparents and ancestors those before me, who have paved the way for me to do what I am called to do. For the continued and never ending support, I thank each and every one of you.

Finally, thank you to the village: Linda Moten-Elliot, Tony Thomson, Jennifer Noonan Ordway and Dr. Mamie Thorns. My coaches: Coach Duncan, Coach Mike Frierson, Coach Calvert, Ms. Calvert, Ms. Malloy, Rekenna Stanford, Coach Hue Martin Robinson, Coach Coulson, Coach Ruffin, Coach Thompson, Coach Johnson, Coach Sparky McEwen,

Coach Farr, Coach Stokes, Coach Marte Smith, Coach Otto Brannum, Coach Jerry Dutcher, Mel Atkins, Mr. Bailey, Coach Curt Andrews, Coach Schulte, Coach Awry, Coach Bobby Williams, Coach Douglas and Coach Ken Mannie. My spiritual mentors and the pastors who ministered to me along the way: Reverend Charles Hudson, Jerry Bishop, Quentin "Q" Henry, Joe Jones, Harold Allaway and Denise Fase. My GRCC Family; My teachers: Ms. Koole, Mrs. Jones, Ms. McCollum, Ms. Jones, Ms. Durham, Mrs. Sturdivant, Mr. Klan, Mrs. Ike, Ms. Chandler, Ms. Widdis (RIP), Mr. Bronson, Mrs. Vaughn-Stepter, Ms. Kenyon and Mrs. Jones. My professors: Mursalata Muhammad, Eric Williams, Vanessa Brooks-Herd, Bart W. Miles, Julie Parks, John VanElst, John Cowles, Shari L. Robinson-Lynk, Stephen J. Yanca (RIP) and Lucy Mercier. Each of you was instrumental to me throughout this journey. You all have helped me become an advanced learner, a responsible young adult, improved my mental toughness and shown me that anything is possible with God.

About the Author

Chris Sain Jr. is an urban young professional who possesses the perfect blend of street smarts, book smarts and common sense. A former Michigan State University student-athlete (football), he is also a renowned speaker, community leader and educator. He graduated at the top of his class with a BSW from Saginaw Valley State University and a MSW from Wayne State University. He is also the CEO and Co-founder of Grand C.I.T.Y. Sports, Inc. a faith based, community driven, non-profit organization in Grand Rapids, MI where he targets at-risk youth by emphasizing education through sports.

www.grandcitysports.com

To book Chris Sain Jr.
please call 616-813-9878
or email chrissainjr@gmail.com

www.chrissain.com

www.ingramcontent.com/pod-product-compliance
Lightning Source LLC
Chambersburg PA
CBHW060920040426
42445CB00011B/711